HAPPY HEALTHY *and* WHOLE

HAPPY HEALTHY and WHOLE

Making Relationships Work

PAULA WHITE CAIN

Copyright © 2021 by Paula White Cain

All rights reserved. No part of this publication can be reproduced, stored in a retrievable system, or transmitted, in any form or by any means electronic, mechanical, photocopying, recording, or otherwise, except by the inclusion of brief quotations in a review, without prior permission in writing from the Publisher.

Unless otherwise noted, all Scriptures are taken from the *New King James Version.* Copyright © 1982 by Thomas Nelson, Inc. Used by permission. All rights reserved.

Scriptures noted AMP are taken from Scripture quotations taken from the *Amplified® Bible*, Copyright © 1954, 1958, 1962, 1964, 1965, 1987 by The Lockman Foundation. Used by permission. (www.Lockman.org)

Scriptures noted NLT are taken from the *Holy Bible, New Living Translation,* copyright © 1996. Used by permission of Tyndale House Publishers, Inc., Wheaton, Illinois 60189. All rights reserved.

ISBN 978-1-7327230-5-4

Published by Paula White Enterprises

Paula White Ministries
P.O. Box 585217
Orlando, Florida 32858

You can reach Paula White Ministries on the Internet at www.paulawhite.org.

Literary development and cover/interior design by Koechel Peterson & Associates, Inc., Minneapolis, Minnesota.

Contents

Introduction
"I Don't Get Wholeness" 9

Chapter One
Healthy Relationships and Wholeness 17

Chapter Two
What an Unhealthy Relationship Looks Like 39

Chapter Three
Three Stages in Development and Relationships 51

Chapter Four
A Closer Look at Dysfunction 63

Chapter Five
Where Are Your Scars? 83

Chapter Six
Three Steps to Breaking a Generational Curse 101

Chapter Seven
A New Start in Healthy Relationships 113

Chapter Eight
Nine Keys to Healthy Relationships 135

Chapter Nine
Steps to Interdependence 173

About the Author

Paula White Cain, a best selling author is President of Paula White Ministries and Senior Pastor of City of Destiny in the greater Orlando, FL area. She hosts a worldwide daily TV program, Paula Today, reaching 195 counties with a potential daily audience of 1,583,460,683 people. Paula's commitment to humanity is felt around the globe as she reaches out through numerous charities and compassion ministries fulfilling her mission to transform lives, heal hearts and win souls. She and her husband, Jonathan Cain live in Apopka, FL

You can learn more about Paula, her work and ministry by visiting Paulawhite.org.

INTRODUCTION

HAPPY HEALTHY
and WHOLE

When Jill was introduced to Charley by friends from their church, she was surprised that such a handsome guy wasn't dating anyone. The more she got to know him, the more she was charmed by his need for care and nurturing. Jill was strong and energetic, and it felt good to be wanted and needed. When Charley asked her to marry him, she couldn't have been more thrilled, even though some of her friends were concerned and thought they were rushing things.

The first six months of their marriage was happy, but soon Jill noticed that Charley's expectations of her were growing in intensity. She discovered that Charley had grown up in a home filled with shame, and he could never measure up to his father's standards. He hadn't pursued a college education because his father had drilled it into him that he'd never make the grade. In truth, Charley was afraid he lacked the ability to hold a job and earn a living, and thought he'd better marry someone who could provide for him. That someone was Jill.

By their first wedding anniversary, Charley had become more and more emotionally dependent upon Jill. He wanted her life to revolve around him and his needs. And he began to demand that she tell him where she was every minute of the day. If she went anywhere, he would telephone her constantly, and if she didn't answer, he would get angry.

When Jill told Charley he had to stop, he tried to restrict her comings and goings by shaming and manipulating her into believing that his obsessive behavior was merely a reflection of his love and concern for her. She, he reasoned, should be just as deeply devoted to him. After all, they were "one," he told her.

With time, Charley cut off the few relationships he had with other friends and saw Jill as the sole source of his worth. He believed he could not live without her. He was exploitive, possessive, and jealous. When Jill's friends got too close, he became rude and offensive, trying and succeeding at alienating her relationships. Jill felt as though she was being suffocated, and there were moments when he made her afraid.

"I Came That They May Have and Enjoy Life"

Charley and Jill highlight the fact that relationships are modeled and passed down to us from our parents and early caregivers. Unless we consciously seek to expand and change these models. We act from within the love and choices we have seen and experienced. Relationships are absolutely vital to the development of the whole person. Whether we consciously realize it or not, everything in our life pivots around our relationships. Everything. God created us as relational beings, and none of us were designed to function independently of others. As you'll see throughout this book, He created us to be interdependent, and our success fulfillment in life will be determined by how we function in this way. I have often said that relationships are the currency of God's Kingdom. God is concerned about every area of our life. He gave us His incredible instruction manual, the Bible, that covers all of life . . . the spiritual, physical, emotional, and financial aspects of our life. It is the greatest "how to" manual ever written. God cares about us in practical ways. He isn't only concerned about us making it into heaven, but He cares about the whole you and me. You were designed to live 100 percent of love and 100 percent of love is available to you.

Jesus said, "He who believes in Me, as the Scripture has said, out of his heart will flow rivers of living water" (John 7:38). We were designed by God to be a well of life. We were designed to be a vessel that gives out from all that is stored up inside of us. Living water, the fullness of the Holy Spirit living inside of us, is to flow freely from us. We were created to walk in prosperity, health, wholeness, joy, peace, provision and vital relationships.

> **"Only when we are comfortable with who we are can we truly function independently in a healthy way, can we truly function within a relationship. Two halves do not make a whole when it comes to a healthy relationship: it takes two wholes."**
> —PATRICIA FRY

God did not create us to feel bad about ourselves. God did not create us to just barely make it through life. God created us to walk in joy and to live a Spirit-filled life. God created us to have a life overflowing with His joy, peace and love. God created us to walk in abundant life. He created us to be Happy, Healthy and Whole.

Jesus said, "The thief comes only in order to steal and kill and destroy. I came that they may have and enjoy life, and have it in abundance (to the full, till it overflows)" (John 10:10 AMP). Let your mind begin to imagine what this means. Jesus Christ came to this earth and gave His life that you could walk in the abundant life and enjoy life to its fullest. But most of us are damaged and fragmented in ways similar to Charley and Jill. Many of us have been wounded by damaging relationships that affected our perceptions of who we are, of others, and particularly of God and His love. Perhaps people have hurt us, neglected us, abandoned us, abused us, violated us, and taken advantage of us. It may have been a severe father, a negligent mother, a contentious sibling, a harsh schoolteacher, or a disloyal spouse.

These damaging relationships leave behind a residue of lies and misbeliefs that handicap us. It is not enough for Jill to tell Charley to just stop his dependent behavior and grow up. Charley cannot give away what he does not possess. He cannot give out life if he doesn't have life. He cannot be what he is not. He cannot function effectively in a role he has no knowledge of or life skills to succeed in.

All of us want fulfillment, significance, validation, respect and love. While some aspects of these desires are going to be impacted by "externals," we aren't going to be "complete" in another relationship, in money, in a career, in the church, in a title, in a fine car, in a new dress or a fancy suit. You don't get that kind of fulfillment from "externals." Instead, if you seek fulfillment in those things solely, you will find yourself frustrated, bankrupt, empty, and void.

The truth is that until we become healthy and whole and healed, we will not be happy and cannot give or receive true love from someone. We cannot give what we don't have. We cannot give others wholeness if we are broken. In order to give something, we must first possess it. In order to love others, we must first love ourselves. And to truly love ourselves, we have to have the love of God in our hearts. God wants to do a work within our life that will then begin to positively impact and affect our relationships.

Fortunately for Jill and Charley, they were able to get help through wise pastoral counseling before their marriage was seriously damaged. Jill thought it was all Charley's problem, which was why she gladly agreed to participate in the counseling sessions. She was surprised to discover she had issues to deal with that played straight into Charley's dependencies.

When the counselor demonstrated to Charley the difference between how he was treating Jill and how a healthy, whole husband would treat her, he took his glasses off, shook his head, and said, "I know that what I do is messed up. I've made her my everything, and that's wrong. But I have no idea how to become healthy."

The counselor nodded his head, smiled, and said, "All of us suffer or have suffered from some sort of trauma or past experiences Charley. The good news is that you see it now . . . and when you can identify the need for help to move from dysfunction to developing healthy relationships, God has a way to restore you, reveal to you what you need, and make you whole."

We all want wholeness.
We want to be satisfied.
We want to be fulfilled.
We want to be happy.

Jeremiah 29:11 God says, I know the plans I've made for you, and they're good plans, plans not to harm you not to do you evil, but to give you hope and prosper you.

God's got a good plan for you.

Psalm 68:19 declares He carries our burdens and loads us up with his benefits and blessings every single day.

Remember who you are. Remember who God is. Remember what God has done. And remember no matter what broke you, no matter what made you fall off the wall - maybe all the king's horses and all the king's men couldn't put you back together again. But the King, God in His Word, and the working of the Holy Spirit, surely can.

His desire is for you to be Happy, Healthy and Whole and my desire is to help you get there!

Love,

Paula

CHAPTER ONE

Healthy Relationships *and* Wholeness

Do you ever look back and wonder about the broken friendships or the broken work relationships or the broken dating relationships or the broken marriage or marriages in your life? Perhaps you're a parent of adult children with whom you're not talking. Or perhaps you're at odds with your parents. Relationships are worth wondering about and getting the right "tools" to build properly.

Despite what you may have experienced so far in life, healthy, vital, joyful, loving relationships are possible. They are not for a select few of God's luckiest saints. That you experience healthy relationships is God's will for your life . . . and His will for everyone's life.

I believe that if you are given the life skills, and if you allow God's love to come into your heart, and if you are taught and apply the Word of God correctly, you will be equipped to enjoy satisfying relationships. God can take any situation, repair it, and restore it when He is invited to do so. It will take work but the rewards of a fulfilling relationship are well worth the effort.

Healthy relationships are found where you have two healed, healthy individuals who function as one together. This is true in every context of our relationships, whether it's with a spouse, a parent, a child, a teacher, a pastor, or an employer. No matter what the functionality of the relationship, the principles in this book will help you build the healthy relationships God wants you to enjoy.

Neale Donald Walsch said, "The purpose of a relationship is not to have another who might complete you, but to have another with whom you might share your completeness." This is crucial for you to understand. It is two people who are whole and healthy, sharing their completeness.

When we are not whole or healthy, the following

words of Tom Robbins clearly sum up what our relationships look like: "When we're incomplete, we're always searching for somebody to complete us. When, after a few years or a few months of a relationship, we find we're still unfulfilled, we blame our partners and take up with somebody more promising. This can go on and on—series polygamy—until we admit that while a partner can add sweet dimensions to our life, we, each of us, are responsible for our own fulfillment. Nobody else can provide it for us, and to believe otherwise is to delude ourselves dangerously and to program for eventual failure in every relationship we enter." No one else can complete you, but they can complement you.

A healthy relationship, on the other hand, is a relationship in which there is balance. There is give and take and mutual appreciation and a building up of each other. It is one in which honest words of appreciation are exchanged without any hint of manipulation or improper motive. It is one of mutual admiration and respect.

There are six components that make for a healthy relationship:

1. I can be me.
2. You can be you.
3. We can be us.
4. I can grow.
5. You can grow.
6. We can grow.

In a healthy relationship, you are free to be yourself even though you may not yet know who you fully are. You see, acquiring self-knowledge is a lifelong process. When God spoke to Adam and Eve after they had fallen into sin, the first thing He said was, "Where are you?" (Genesis 3:9). In essence, He said, "Adam, find yourself. Eve, locate yourself. Who are you? Where are you?" And that discovery of finding out who we are is something that evolves in our life. We are continually discovering ourselves as we mature in God and grow in life. Some relationships are meant for life, some are seasonal, all should be causing us to grow, even the ones that ended in ways that you did not desire.

> "Love creates an 'us' without destroying a 'me.'"
> —LEO BUSCAGLIA

A healthy relationship is where we grow together by developing mutual goals, working together to achieve them. Healthy relationships come along with people who have a common direction or destination—common values and goals. If you do not have a common direction, you will always be in conflict. And interestingly enough, it is not the goals that are achieved that make the relationship healthy. It is the journey toward the goals, and not the goals themselves, that causes you to grow. It's making sure you pay attention to the details and never stop acquiring knowledge of the other individual. Remember, they are transforming continually.

Wholeness

Mother Teresa said, "God has created us *to love and to be loved,* and this is the beginning of prayer—to know that He loves me, that I have been created for greater things." Isn't that what we all desire really, to know that someone loves, accepts, and values us? It's the core of our essence. It is the foundation. And did you know studies have revealed that if you know you are loved by one person, just one, it brings forth a confidence that you can do anything?

However, we often make the mistake of depending upon other people to love us, and when they fail to give that love in the way we expect, we are left empty and unfulfilled. But you don't have to wait for somebody else to give you that love. It can be discovered in yourself by the love of God that is your firm foundation. When you choose to engage in the process of knowing and cultivating your spiritual self you can then truly direct yourself to love and to all that is good and God. You are not a victim who must wait for somebody else to validate you. It is wonderful to receive love from others, but you are capable of giving that love you desire to yourself. I'm going to show you the way to wholeness, where you become complete and complementary to stand next to a person and have whole functional relationships.

To have healthy relationships requires that we are healthy, whole people. And the only one who can bring us to wholeness and healing is God. "Now may the God of peace Himself sanctify you completely; and may your whole spirit, soul, and body be preserved blameless at the coming of our Lord Jesus Christ. He who calls you is faithful, who also will do it" (1 Thessalonians 5:23–24).

When the Bible declares, "Now may the God of peace . . . ," keep in mind that *peace* means "wholeness." The apostle Paul is saying, "May the very God of wholeness sanctify you wholly, and I pray God your whole spirit, soul, and body be preserved blameless until the coming of our Lord Jesus Christ." And part of your wholeness is linked to the development of healthy relationships.

Relationships are vital to the development of the whole person. A central contributor to most psychological disorders is the core feeling of disconnectedness. Psychologists tell us that our self-concept is largely developed by the most important person in our life— how they see us. Obviously, that can be good, if that person is healthy and whole and loving and kind. But if that person is messed up, how they see us and how they treat us can mess us up. And it's often damaging to have a person as a role model who doesn't know how to model the role they are placed in. How can a person be a role model if they have never had a model for the role they are now responsible to be?

It makes me think of Eve. People talk about Adam and Eve and say, "If they wouldn't have messed everything up, I wouldn't have all these problems I'm facing today." And most of the blame they try to pin on Eve. Personally, I feel sorry for Eve. Put yourself in her position. She just came to life one day and saw Adam's smiling face as he said, "Honey, get me my socks and cook me some grits." Day one on the planet and she's got the role of a wife without a pastor, counselor, teacher, mentor, or mother to explain what it means to be a wife. That's hard! No wonder the girl went on a long walk and lent her ear to Satan. Have some sympathy for this woman and man who never had models for the roles they were given. It's not easy to walk down a path that has never been traveled.

I think you'll agree we often share this same problem. We are placed in positions we've never been empowered to perform. Our father or mother may not have been the role models we needed. How do you or I successfully function in a relationship without the necessary tools and skills? The good news is you are not stuck. You can be equipped with the skills and tools that will access your God-given ability to love and to respond to love.

Loving God, Loving Others

The first principle toward healthy relationships is that in order to love others, I must first love myself. And in order to love myself, I must know the love of God. It all begins with the greatest commandment as taught by

Jesus: " 'You shall love the LORD your God with all your heart, with all your soul, and with all your mind.' This is the first and great commandment. And the second is like it: 'You shall love your neighbor as yourself.' On these two commandments hang all the Law and the Prophets" (Matthew 22:37–40).

How can I love someone else if I don't even love myself? Relationships that function best and are fulfilling start with two people who have healthiness, wholeness, completeness within their own lives. It requires two people who are whole, who understand who they are in God and who they are in themselves. Out of their wholeness or fullness, they are able to make that relationship work and to maximize it to its greatest potential. So if I'm going to love myself, I had better understand the love of God.

"Beloved, let us love one another, for love is (springs) from God; and he who loves [his fellowmen] is begotten (born) of God and is coming [progressively] to know and understand God [to perceive and recognize and get a better and clearer knowledge of Him]" (1 John 4:7 AMP). According to the apostle John, the more I get to know and understand God, the more I have a capability of loving.

John adds this thought: "He who does not love has not become acquainted with God [does not and never did know Him], for God is love" (v. 8). So it's through our relationship with God that we have the ability to establish the foundation of love. And the Bible teaches us that if the foundation is destroyed, what will the righteous do (Psalm 11:3)? If you have no foundation, then you have nothing to build upon. According to the Word of God, love is your foundation based upon your relationship with God. When I love, I put Gods love into action. I engage in a supernatural act from my spirit. When I do this I know God. God is love, and to be truly loving is to be like God in His nature.

Studies have proven that long-term happiness in life is best achieved by those who have the ability to give and receive love unconditionally. God's love is unconditional, and our love is to be the same. "Unconditional love" means we choose to love even though there are imperfections in people's lives that we wish were otherwise. To love unconditionally says, "I love you in spite of you. I love you with all your weaknesses, your flaws, and your strengths." God wants every true good for everyone at all times.

What you focus on is going to make a difference in the functionality of your relationship. To love others is a choice, and to do so unconditionally means to accept every aspect of that person, recognizing that the landscape of their life has been affected by their life experience—by the people in their life and by what's happened. You also recognize that they are being changed from glory to glory as they get to know God (2 Corinthians 3:18). Transformation is a lifelong process of growth. For our part, we have a greater degree of love because we are daily growing in our knowledge of God. Every day we are focusing on knowing God more than we knew Him yesterday, which means every day we're going to walk in a deeper depth and dimension of the love of God. You are the only person that can hinder your progress to deepen your ability to love and to be loved.

Relationships function best when a person becomes whole. Wholeness, fulfillment, and satisfaction come first by acknowledging and receiving God's love, and then you have the ability to love and accept yourself. To do this, commit to explore the truths within your innermost self without fear or judgment. Ask God to enlighten and reveal His truth to you. And out of that inner fullness and a wholeness you can begin to love and accept others.

Consider these words from Ephesians 3:16–18 in the *Amplified Bible*:

> *May He grant you out of the rich treasury of His glory to be strengthened and reinforced with mighty power in the inner man by the [Holy] Spirit [Himself indwelling your innermost being and personality]. May Christ through your faith [actually] dwell (settle down, abide, make His permanent home) in your hearts! May you be rooted deep in love and founded securely on love, that you may have the power and*

be strong to apprehend and grasp with all the saints [God's devoted people, the experience of that love] what is the breadth and length and height and depth [of it].

I can never have fullness in my life until I possess the knowledge of God's love for me. And this is not based on head knowledge or intelligence; it's based on an intimate experience of God. Until I become intimate with God and really know who I am in Christ, I will struggle to be something I was never created to be. And while most of us are waiting for something from the outside to fix us on the inside, to make us right, it doesn't come from the outside— it comes from the inside.

For instance, if we are asking God to give us a brilliant career, we've got it backward. A brilliant career doesn't start by something outside of us. *Greatness* doesn't start on the outside. It starts by discovering the brilliancy within. When you find what you were created for and figure out a way to wrap your living around the passion that God birthed on the inside of you, then your brilliant career

> "Oh, the comfort, the inexpressible comfort of feeling safe with a person, having neither to weigh thoughts nor measure words, but pouring them all out, just as they are, chaff and grain together, certain that a faithful hand will take and sift them, keep what is worth keeping, and with a breath of kindness blow the rest away."
>
> —DINAH CRAIK

is birthed forth. So it is with virtually all externals. They complement who you really are but don't define you.

We have to stop looking for something from the outside to fix what's on the inside. People have a free will. Choose to respect the individual freedom of a person that you are wanting to give you love, or worse, trying to control or manipulate them for something you desire. Each person has his or her own personal opportunity to choose or reject love. If someone chooses to put off conscious loving, that doesn't mean you have to put it off in your life. Instead of using your energy to try and change them, redirect it to loving and changing yourself. God Himself does not force His love on us. Allow God's love to pierce through any pain you carry and heal any hurt. When you can shut life down and stop all the noise long enough to discern who you really are, when you can hear the voice of God speaking truth to your inner man, then you begin to function fully because you understand: *I am valuable. I am worthy. I am a treasure.*

There is great comfort when you don't have to perform for acceptance, wear a false mask, or live a guarded life, but you can freely stand before others with a confidence in who you genuinely are.

Do You Know Who You Are?

So who are you? Are you healthy and whole . . . or unhealthy and incomplete? You cannot overcome your condition until you know your position. You really don't know who you are until you discover it through your relationship with God through His Son Jesus Christ.

The apostle Paul states our position this way: "Therefore, if anyone is in Christ, he is a new creation; old things have passed away; behold, all things have become new" (2 Corinthians 5:17). Until you realize who you are *in* Christ, you'll continue to produce the same unhealthy behavior that matches your old belief system. That's why Jesus said you can't put new wine in old wineskins (Matthew 9:17). Both will be ruined.

The Greek word for *in*, when referring to being *in Christ*, denotes a position of relationship and rest. The only way you can ever overcome your unhealthy condition is by knowing who you are in Jesus Christ.

Knowing "church" doesn't change you.

Knowing Hebrew and Greek doesn't change you.

Even knowing Bible verses doesn't change you if they are only in your head and not in your heart.

Only knowing Christ and your position in Him changes you! When you know who He is, then you can know who you are in Him.

To be a "new creation" in Christ means "to be recently made, unused, fresh, and unprecedented." The old has passed away. It means your spirit man is changed, and with that spirit change that comes, God illuminates you. He shows you a picture of who you are. You are no longer a sinner. You may still have issues dealing with sin, but now you have the righteousness of Christ—you are in right standing with God. One of the translations of "righteousness" is "clear self." You are "clear with God." When you know this truth, your behavior starts to line up with it. Behavior is simply a manifestation of belief.

> **"It is possible to be different and still be all right."**
> —ANNE WILSON SCHAEF

Knowing your position in Christ Jesus gives you the power to overcome any condition related to your past. When you know your position, your old "condition" has no power over you. You will have the power to straighten up on the inside and on the outside. You will have a new posture, a new bearing, a new dignity. When you begin to understand who loves you and who has adopted you into His family, you'll discover a new way to look, to think, to talk, to walk, to act, and to respond to life. He frees you to fully live out His design for your life. God is infinite, so His love is infinite. Because it is limitless, you can never absorb all the love God has to offer you.

YOU ARE FEARFULLY AND WONDERFULLY MADE

Psalm 139:14 is a powerful verse I hope you've memorized. "I will praise You, for I am fearfully and wonderfully made; marvelous are Your works, and that my soul knows very well." When you understand the depths of this verse, you'll never have to have a worship leader get you pumped up for praising God again. You won't need someone to coax you to worship with your whole heart. Worship comes as a natural result of understanding that you are "fearfully and wonderfully made."

The word *fearfully* means I am "reverently" created in the image of God. Do you understand how amazing that is? That means the same God who created everything from nothing also placed His image or likeness in your life. And if you believe in Jesus Christ, He is now living in your life! That's the Almighty One who spoke and all things came into existence by the power of His word (Hebrews 11:3). You are reverently made in the image of God. When you understand you are made with value that is priceless, you won't violate what you value.

Indeed, you are also *wonderfully* made. To be *wonderful* means you're "different or unique." It means to "set apart, to distinguish, to be marked out, to be distinct." What makes you so great is that you are different from everybody else. There is no one else like you. Nobody has your set of fingerprints, and no one ever will. There will never be anyone who has your DNA. You have the perfect package for all that the Master Architect designed you to be. Your ears are just the way they should be. Your body shape and blood type are perfect. That personality of yours is all yours, and it's beautiful.

When I was growing up, they called me "M&M," for "Motormouth." My first-grade teacher made me stand in the corner of the classroom for talking too much, and I did talk a lot. I can still hear her say, "Paula might be something if she ever learns to shut her mouth." I did not realize at the time that the devil was telling me my destiny. Had I believed her words, my purpose would never have been fulfilled. My mouth was my gift, through which I would one day communicate the Word of God. I was designed to have a mouth that could out-talk anybody. I just had to learn how to use it for the right purposes, to be constructive and not destructive with it. To be timely and seasoned in my words. To be developed.

Everything about you is precisely and perfectly created and put together. To be *wonderfully* made means you are all that and a bag of chips. (I've written a book *You Are All That*, which takes you on a deep journey to discover or recover your authentic self and align your life with the desires God has for you.) It means no one can duplicate you. God is the one who made you. God is the one who put everything together. You are different, and that's what makes you so valuable. You are a rare artifact of immeasurable value.

When you accept who you are, you give yourself one of life's greatest gifts. Why would you want to mess with the perfection of God, anyway? He knew what He was doing when He created you. Man's opinion has no value or authority against the decisions of God. He designed you and fashioned your life for a tailor-made fit!

And when you discover your real value and build a life based on your uniqueness, no one can take your place. No one can be you. The whole dynamics of your life change.

Unfortunately, most people don't realize their value, and as a result they're trying to be a cookie-cutter mold of everything else they see. But you are a Designer's original, so why would you settle for being a cheap imitation?

David said, "I am fearfully and wonderfully made; marvelous are Your works, and that my soul knows very well." Does your soul—your mind, your will, and your emotions—know "very well" that you are fearfully and wonderfully made? If you don't, don't wait another second to come to this understanding.

I can tell you this much: my soul "knows" this "very well." That might sound arrogant, but it's not. It is simply the confidence I have gained from digging into the depths of the Word. God has shown me I'm not a product of what I went through in life. I am not what people said about me, and I did not necessarily deserve what they did to me. *I am a creation of an Almighty God.* That is not to take responsibility off the actions I created that caused the consequences I must now walk through. It is to say, man's decisions, right or wrong for my life, cannot stop His destiny or determination for me.

We *must* base our personal esteem solely on the fact that God has "precision-ally," precisely and perfectly, put us together. If not, we will spend a lifetime trying to be something we were never created to be. And neither you nor I will ever be our authentic selves. NEVER. NOT POSSIBLE. And until you are authentic to yourself, you will never find your real value.

Remember: your greatness is found in your differences, your uniqueness. When you discover God's love, then you can begin to build on a firm foundation to respect and love yourself. And when you love yourself, you can begin to love others. You can only give what you have. You can only release a genuine, healthy love to others from the love of God inside you.

When you recognize and accept your uniqueness, you cease jealous behavior toward others and start celebrating your differences. Jealousy is rooted in the fear that you can be replaced. You need to come to understand that you can stand next to another person, and they can never replace you. That person may be in an advanced position of you or possess more than you, but they can never be you. You can feel good about yourself! Stop competing with others, and start completing. You are unique, so celebrate!

You cannot be an effective vessel for God in this world if you have a damaged view of God's love. It's similar to what happened to Jonathan's son Mephibosheth, who as a five-year-old child was dropped by his nurse, whom he loved and trusted, and ended up being crippled in both feet (2 Samuel 4:4). When people who love us also damage us, we get a distorted view of God. We begin to look at God through the eyes of man instead of looking at man through the eyes of God.

We have to realize that God will not fail, hurt, or abandon us as the men and women in our life do, whether they hurt us intentionally or unintentionally. Note that Jesus did not put His trust in man, for He knew what is in our hearts. "But Jesus did not commit Himself to them, because He knew all men, and had no need that anyone should testify of man, for He knew what was in man" (John 2:24–25). Our ultimate trust and complete reliance must be in God alone.

As I trust God, then I can also trust that God will do what He needs to do *in* me and those who are connected to my life so that a mutual love and respect can be reciprocated. However, if I put my trust or reliance in that person, they will often fail and let me down at some point, because men and women are not capable of being God. We are imperfect people who are growing and changing continually. There is only one God in my life. There is only one Person who can love me unconditionally. There is only one Person who completely knows me, and He is God. I must "put God first" and seek first His kingdom if I want to be whole and healthy and release the abundant life He has for me (Matthew 6:33). To be wholly loved, we must become whole again. This is a process of taking the fragmented parts of our life, our disconnected and scattered selves and putting them back in their original place. Basically, this process is about piecing back together the parts of ourselves that were rejected, abandoned and wounded in our childhood. It's about reintegrating and accepting the parts of you that got "dropped" like Mephibosheth. Those are the wounds that made you stop functioning and developing properly. Everything from being told you were useless, or bad, or worthless, or stupid. I want you to really listen to the place deep within you that is crying out and feels profound pain and invite God to bring His love and healing.

You Are God's Workmanship

Here's another life-transforming verse you need to memorize and meditate upon. The apostle Paul said, "For we are His workmanship, created in Christ Jesus for good works, which God prepared beforehand that we should walk in them" (Ephesians 2:10).

The Greek word for *workmanship* means "product." You are the product of the Almighty God. You were not an accident or a mistake, even if your unwed parents spent a night of passion at a motel to conceive you. God was not caught off-guard. You were purposed and planned in God's heart and mind long before they came together.

When you begin to understand that, you'll see that life is a gift, and God gifted life through you and to you.

God used your parents to bring you into this earthly realm, but He is your Creator. He packaged together everything, wrapping your soul and body around your spirit. Despite whatever damage or injury you may have experienced in your soul or body, this does not deter from the purpose of God for your life for which He has designed your personality and "package" to fit precisely.

We are God's workmanship, created "in Christ Jesus for good works." In other words, you are a product of God, and you were purposed through your faith relationship of resting in Jesus Christ to do good works, which means "well or beneficial deeds" toward others. And God has preordained we should walk in them. Obviously, I must come to an understanding of who I am in Christ to walk out the life God has purposed for me. When I know who I am, then I know what I can do. I know what I can do through my relationship with God and His revealed Word to me.

To Change Your Behavior, Change Your Beliefs

Here's the principle that underlies all you do: *your behavior stems from your belief system.* If I am going to change my behavior, I have to change my beliefs. I'm sure it's just as true for you as it was for me: life lied to me, and I believed the lies, and I acted accordingly.

Life told me I couldn't have it.
Life told me I couldn't do it.
Life told me I was a victim.

Life told me my daddy killed himself because he didn't love me.

Life told me I wasn't worth much, which is why I was sexually abused.

> "Marriage is not a ritual or an end. It is a long, intricate, intimate dance together, and nothing matters more than your own sense of balance and your choice of a partner."
> —AMY BLOOM

All of those terrible lies and messages that kept repeating in my life were shattered and their power broken when I found out I am not a product of what I went through. I am a product of what God says about me! I found out I did not have to have a victim mentality, or be poor in soul or spirit the rest of my life, or be on the down and out. God changed the message and spoke into my life: "I can do all things through Christ Jesus who strengthens me" (Philippians 4:13). My behavior changed as the message changed my life.

Whatever your behavior is in a relationship, realize it stems from the fundamental beliefs you hold. Change the message, and you'll change your life. God's Word cannot do less than transform you when you believe it.

CHAPTER TWO

What *an* Unhealthy Relationship Looks Like

Now, in order to understand healthy relationships, which is our goal, we have to discern what is not healthy. We have to look at both aspects of relationship. Developing a role model for unhealthy relationships will help us discern what is dysfunctional in our life.

Genesis 29 tells the story of how the patriarch Isaac sent his son Jacob back to his people to find a wife from among his wife's family. Rebekah, Jacob's mother, had a brother Laban, who had two daughters, Leah and Rachel. Jacob fell head over heels in love with the shapely and beautiful Rachel, so Laban struck a deal that if Jacob worked for Laban for seven years he could marry Rachel. Apparently Leah was a "Plain Jane," but Rachel was a knockout.

However, after seven years of labor, Laban managed to trick Jacob into marrying Leah first. It was a relationship conceived in deception, and anything birthed in deception will produce deception. Jacob loved Rachel passionately, and he did not love Leah. She was caught in a web of deception that was not of her doing.

Leah was a victim in every sense of the word and in all of her relationships. All she ever wanted was what all women want—to be loved. She craved affection. She wanted to be admired and respected for who she was.

It's the same with us. We want our parents to love and respect us. We want our spouse, our children, our friends, and our coworkers to validate, admire and love us. We want someone . . . anyone . . . in our life who will affirm us and love us unconditionally.

That's what Leah wanted . . . but it is not what Leah got.

Leah knew she was not the wife whom Jacob wanted. So she began her efforts to win Jacob's love and affection. Leah wanted this relationship to work, and she was determined to do what she could to win the heart of her husband who did not want her. So she started having children, thinking if she produced sons for Jacob, he would love her.

> When the LORD saw that Leah was unloved, He opened her womb; but Rachel was barren. So Leah conceived and bore a son, and she called his name Reuben; for she said, "The LORD has surely looked on my affliction. Now therefore, my husband will love me." Then she conceived again and bore a son, and said, "Because the LORD has heard that I am unloved, He has therefore given me this son also." And she called his name Simeon. She conceived again and bore a son, and said, "Now this time my husband will become attached to me, because I have borne him three sons." Therefore his name was called Levi. And she conceived again and bore a son, and said, "Now I will praise the LORD." Therefore she called his name Judah. Then she stopped bearing.
>
> GENESIS 29:31–35

LEAH HAD SET UP IDOLS THAT KEPT HER FROM WHOLENESS

With Leah as our example of unhealthy relationships, I may surprise you by stating that the starting point for turning unhealthy relationships into healthy relationships is eliminating the idols in your life and putting God first. Read Leah's story again carefully. Even though Leah had a covenant and a relationship with God, and she birthed blessings given to her by God, she did it for a wrong reason. She kept birthing the blessing of God, but she proceeded to use it to parade around for the affection of Jacob. She kept producing something good, but she did it with a wrong motive. Motives are what incite you to action.

Here's the principle: if you birth a blessing and use it for the wrong purpose, it will always leave you empty and going back for what you want and are never satisfied to get. It becomes a sick cycle you will repeat and repeat and repeat.

Leah genuinely wanted the love and attention of Jacob, which was not wrong. But there was a component to it in her life that turned it into an obsession. The love and affection she desired from Jacob, who was not capable of giving it to her, became her god—an idol.

Today, we think of gods or idols as statues or little men with round bellies. But an idol can be anything to which you give your worship. It is anything toward which you pay excessive attention or focus. An idol is anything toward which you yield your strength or the best part of you.

I realize that most of us have not built a shrine in our house or our office or workplace, but that does not eliminate the fact that many of us have idols in our life. Do you realize you can worship another person or some thing by paying too much attention to them or it? It can become an idol if you dedicate your life to impress them. It can be an idol if you are using it to try to receive your validation or value from that person or position or thing.

For instance, I've met women who work out six hours a day because they're so afraid their man is going to see and pursue another woman who has a better body than theirs. They've become obsessed with holding on to their husband's approval, and that has become an idol. Your value does not come from the person to whom you're married or your parents or your job or the neighborhood you live in. Your value comes from the Lord and the covenant you have with Him.

Anything can become an idol in our life.
Money can become an idol.
A child can become an idol.
A hobby can become an idol.
A church, yes, your church, can become an idol.
Here is God's Word to us:

"You shall have no other gods before Me. You shall not make for yourself a carved image—any likeness of anything that is in heaven above, or that is in the earth beneath, or that is in the water under the earth; you shall not bow down to them nor serve them. For I, the Lord *your God, am a jealous God, visiting the*

iniquity of the fathers upon the children to the third and fourth generations of those who hate Me."

—Exodus 20:3–5

God would say to Leah as He says to us, "Let's start by getting your life in order. Let's prioritize. I don't mind you having all these great blessings in your life. In fact, I want them to be richly abundant. But the only way they become great is if I am your God."

> **"The greatest happiness of life is the conviction that we are loved—loved for ourselves, or rather, loved in spite of ourselves."**
> —VICTOR HUGO

Leah needed to take the same steps we must take. First, she needed to ask herself why she wanted Jacob's love so desperately. We need to examine our life and ask why it is that we do what we do.

Because Leah so wanted Jacob's love, she kept repeating the same sick cycles in her life. Some people call these sick cycles "generational curses," while others call it a "dysfunctional family." Call it whatever you like, but we must deal with it. God gave His Son, Jesus Christ, to be crucified on an old rugged cross, not simply to get us to heaven but to give us freedom, joy, peace, purpose and an abundant life here on earth so we can represent God in the earth today.

Whatever your generational curse is, whatever your dysfunction is, whatever behavior has plagued you and been a problem in your life, it can be broken. I believe

God's Word is going to set you free and give you the necessary instruction and guidance to get you in alignment with the right pathway for your life.

So let's take a closer look at Leah's life and examine the underlying problem to Leah's dysfunction, which often is the heart at our own dysfunction.

Leah's Dysfunction Began With Her Father

Underlying Leah's dysfunction, we see the principle of an unhealthy parent operating in her life. Leah is the daughter of Laban, and his influence and impact on her life are profound. A father's role is to guard, govern, and guide. The significance of this role or lack of it in our life has a deep impression and major effect. Although Jacob was a skilled con man, Laban was more than Jacob's match as a deceiver. Jacob did not realize there is always somebody who can out-con the con, and Laban was a little more accomplished in his skills as a con man. Even Jacob never dreamed a father would use his daughter as a "booby prize" to get what he wanted.

Over the years, I have been amazed by the large number of women or young ladies I have met who ended up in a relationship or married to a man who is significantly like their father. If a daughter, such as Leah or you or me, does not have a healthy relationship with her father (or mother), where she receives esteem, affection, and validation from him, she will often try to get those unfulfilled inner needs met through a relationship with a man who will be very much like her father. I see so many women in this position of trying to get in their adult life what was missing in their childhood. Our parents modeled a range of choices for us through how they related to each other, other people and us. They passed down to us the behaviors they learned from their parents. For example, if they modeled coping mechanisms of excessive drinking, abandonment or leaving, you may think there are only two ways to deal with problems. You will continue to model these behavior problems until you learn you have other choices. That is why it is imperative to connect with the eternal truths of God and His Word which have the power to break the mold of learned behavior and generational curses. Once you revoke, remove the old and begin to replace it with the new (the truth of God's Word) you begin the process of transformation and start to change the old model.

In Leah's life, the sick cycles started with her father. In her case, she had a father who used her as a pawn in a moment of deception to gain seven more years of labor from Jacob. Leah had a father who did not value or validate her. He was a father who used her and manipulated her for his personal gain. Put yourself in her place and imagine what she felt like.

Watch this carefully. Leah's problem started from her childhood, which she was later forced to deal with as an adult. It is just as true for any of us. In order to see a bit of your future, you're going to have to look to your past, because the problems you deal with as an adult started somewhere in your childhood. In our life it might have been the fact that we had no father, or that our father was physically present but still an absentee. It could be that our mother took on the role of our father. Perhaps it was a sibling who abused us. All of these different dynamics come into play in the family. But ultimately it has a profound impact on every person.

So why does Leah want Jacob so bad? Why does she want his love when he could care less about her? Simple. She wants from Jacob what she did not get as a child from her father. And all of us do the same: we seek what we did not get as a child, and we keep seeking and seeking. In the absence of the recognition of real love, we do crazy things to get someone to love us.

It gets down to the basics of our humanity. When psychologists ask people why they want to be close to another human being, the three most common answers are these:

1. "Because I don't want to be lonely."
2. "Because I don't want to feel unlovable."
3. "Because I don't want to be afraid."

In other words, "I want to be close to someone because I don't want to feel as an adult what I felt as a child. In essence, I want an intimate relationship to fix my childhood."

Now, here's the overwhelming problem with this notion: *another person cannot fix our childhood.* It is not in the realm of possibility. Nevertheless, we create this dynamic of dysfunction that does not and cannot work.

One Word to Fathers

We see in Leah's experience the powerful role that fathers exercise in their children's lives, and I must highlight it as regards to the establishment of healthy relationships. If you are a father or are planning on being a father someday, please take seriously the significant role you play as a male role model in your child's life. Your role in their life is the most important role on the Planet Earth. Your relationship with your child will affect everything in their present and future. Here's why.

God has given man the headship of the family, and everything flows down from them and affects every other relationship in the family. Your delegated authority as head of the family is intrinsic to your manhood, and if you are a healthy and whole man, you can give out of the fullness of your life and affirm and encourage your child's self-esteem and validate them for life. It is one of the tremendous responsibilities and joys of being a father.

In stating the authority of the father, I am not inferring women do not have a position, or women are not significant or are lower in importance than their husbands. But the Bible states the woman is "the glory of the man" (1 Corinthians 11:7). "The glory" means she is "the shadow" of her husband. Whatever he is, she is a part of it. Women have influence, but men have authority. When this is out of order, it creates a dysfunction that causes confusion, identity crisis, and chaos. No matter how much our culture changes, the Word of God remains firm, true and consistent.

A strong church is achieved by strong individuals who are in the proper order of God's divine arrangement. This will require strong godly men. Which is why the enemy has been working overtime to erode and kill the manhood of every male, because if he can weaken or destroy the man, he can affect us all. If the enemy can diminish or eliminate the role of a father in a family, its effects and damage are real and evident. Just survey the moral and cultural landscape of our world today.

Men, healthy relationships in your family start with you. God has called you to be a leader, a protector, a provider, a role model—to be a nurturing husband, lover, and father. Do not regard this responsibility as daunting. You face opposition, struggles, and tough choices. You are presented with opportunities to compromise your beliefs . . . but be encouraged, you can be a man of honor. You are up to the task, and you are highly qualified for this position for which you were chosen before the foundation of the earth.

You are a man of honor, and you can live as one! I respect the role you have fulfilled in being granted headship. I believe that God will give you the wisdom to effectively walk and lead in that position.

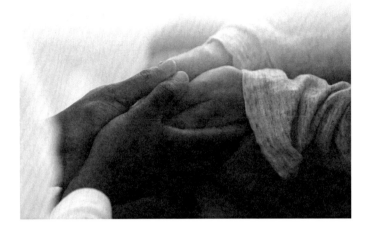

CHAPTER THREE

Three Stages *in* Development *and* Relationships

There are three stages in the development of who you are, and these stages have a profound impact on your relationships. It's vital you understand each stage and determine where you are in relationship to your own personal growth.

Dependence

The first stage in personal development is *dependence*. Your dependence stage is from infancy through childhood. When a child is born, he is totally dependent on his parents and others. This is a stage of nurturing, and it's a proven fact that if a child is isolated, if a child is not nurtured, it will have a devastating impact on their personal formation. It has been stated that a person's personality is formed before he or she is six years old, so the nurturing they are given is critical. The more healthy and whole parents are, the more sure their children are healthy and pass down a healthy heritage.

Comparing this stage to your spiritual life, when you are first born again, you are dependent on other people to a certain degree. You are dependent upon them to teach you and train you about the things of God and show the pathway to spiritual growth. When you first come to faith in Jesus Christ, you're on spiritual milk (1 Peter 2:2; Hebrews 5:12). Somebody is feeding you with a bottle. But you're not to stay on that milk of the Word forever. Ultimately, as you grow, you should be able to take the Word and feed yourself. You should be able to take the solid food of the Word, and one day you are able to chow down on a sirloin and a filet mignon because you are "mature" (Hebrews 5:14).

INDEPENDENCE

The second stage of development is *independence*. This takes place during our adolescent stage. It is that difficult time when a child is moving into independence and breaking some of the bonds of dependence. If you're the parent of teenagers and want to send them away to an island until they're twenty-three, you know what I mean. It's that period when you wonder if someone gave you the wrong baby when you left the hospital.

What happens is the child is moving into independence and toward adulthood. But the move to independence almost always goes too far and often results in rebellion—a standing in a position of self-governing that says "I'm always right." It's all a part of learning to be self-governing, no longer relying on someone else, and not looking for relationships to help build you.

> **"Don't smother each other. No one can grow in the shade."**
> —LEO BUSCAGLIA

In our spiritual lives, when someone is moving from dependency to independence, we see them go from being totally dependent to "I can do this all on my own!" Well, you can't do it all on your own. You need a pastor. You need someone who watches out for you . . . you need accountability . . . you need a prayer partner. God wants us to be dependent upon Him, but there is a healthy place of interdependence He wants us to have in the body of Christ.

During these natural phases of development from dependence to independence to interdependence, many people get messed up and end up in dysfunction.

INTERDEPENDENCE VERSUS CODEPENDENCY

It is healthy and natural for us to move into independence and want to get into interdependence with others. However, many of us did not receive the proper nurturing to fully develop into wholeness, and because we are lacking or have been damaged along the way, we end up in dysfunctional relationships that don't work. Instead of growing into interdependence and healthy relationships, where we are free to love others and to receive love back, we create a codependence that is always unhealthy. You let others direct your life.

The reason so many people don't grow to be healthy personalities can be seen symbolically through a baby's connection to its mother with an umbilical cord. The umbilical cord represents the place where the baby should be nurtured and fed; the place that should bring life to the baby. But if the umbilical cord is severed or somehow gets blocked while the baby is in this totally dependent stage, the baby won't receive the proper nurturing and nutrition required to develop into wholeness.

It's not that the people who were meant to be nurturers in our life wanted or meant to leave us underdeveloped. It's just that hurting people hurt people. If their role models failed them, how do they not fail in the same way? How does a woman know how to be a wife when she's never seen what a healthy wife looks like? How does a man know how to be a good father if his father was a mess?

What happens when our self-esteem or self-worth is underdeveloped is that a dysfunction starts within us, and then our self-worth becomes dependent on external sources. In other words, we look to other people or something outside ourselves to try to make us feel complete and whole.

Codependency is a psychological condition or a relationship in which a person is controlled or manipulated by another person. Here's how you can quickly identify a codependent situation—it's one where your mood is determined by somebody else. You are codependent when how you feel about yourself—your worth or value—is determined by somebody else.

So being codependent is when you begin to get your worth developed by someone else or by externals. It means you are depending on something outside of yourself to provide your sense of well-being. You are always trying to get something on the outside to fill something on the inside, which is totally backward. If you study yourself closely, you'll find your own internal conflicts are the cause of your dysfunctional relationships. When you are confused it refers to blurred boundaries. You no longer identify a clear sense of self, purpose or direction. You don't know where you end, and another person begins. It's like one big bowl of spaghetti and you don't know which noodle you are. You are all bundled together with no separation.

Actually the term *codependency* is inaccurate. A more accurate term would be *outer dependence* or *external dependence,* because it's characterized by a dependence on outer or external sources for self-worth and self-definition. It means you are allowing things on the outside to define who you are.

You have to know the "real you" is nothing external. The real you is not the way you look on the outside or what someone says or thinks about you. Your real worth is your core being, your essence, who you really are, which never changes and has no variables. You have a spirit; you are a spirit. And when I talk about life by design, I'm talking about finding the value of your authentic voice by building a life from the inside out. You are free to live a life by design when you're anchored in who you really are.

That's why you need to know the love of God. Because when you know how much God loves you, the opinion of man to define you has no bearing. You get an attitude that says, "Oh, excuse me. You don't want to celebrate me? Sorry. Next." It's not arrogance but a confidence from a healthy development of self. You can handle rejection if you don't need acceptance from the person rejecting you. You don't waste a lifetime trying to get somebody to like you and love you and celebrate you. That "please, please, please love and care for me" attitude has to be broken. You are not a doormat to allow people to walk all over you.

So codependence and interdependence are two very different dynamics. A healthy relationship moves into interdependence. But codependence is about giving away power over your self-esteem. Here's what the disease of codependency looks like: you keep repeating the same sick cycles and patterns. Rather than break the sick cycles, you keep doing what is familiar, even though it is dysfunctional and harmful.

> "Eighty percent of life's satisfaction comes from meaningful relationships"
> —BRIAN TRACY

In the chapters that follow, I'll go into this more in-depth. But you need to know that if you keep repeating a familiar sick pattern, you will keep picking untrustworthy people to trust. And although you think you're going to get something new and different, it's not going to happen. You'll wonder, *Why do I keep getting the same package in a different gift wrapping—the same type of person who just looks different?* Here's the reason: because there is something in you pulling those things toward you. It's true in your love relationship and friendships as well as in the dynamics of a ministry or work.

Until you change by receiving the revelation of who you really are, your circumstances are not going to change. That's why when you know the love of God—not head knowledge but knowledge based on an independent experience and intimate encounter—He puts His seed in you, and you begin to birth out who you really are.

What Codependency Looked Like in My Life

Here's what codependency looked like before I found my way into interdependence through the love of God. Codependence and a dysfunctional mindset said this to me: "I have to be needed in order to have a relationship with others." I desperately needed to be needed. And people who are codependent will often do just about anything to have someone say to them, "I need you."

When I finally comprehended the love of God and found healing and wholeness, this is the truth that came through loud and clear: I need God. Period. Beyond Him, I might want something, but I don't need it. Because when I need it, it means "I can't live without it. I can't survive without it." As we saw in Leah's life, that's an idol or an addiction, which is destructive to us.

Here's another scenario that reflects being in codependent, dysfunctional relationships. You would assume responsibility for others' feelings and behaviors, which is an easy signal to spot in codependents. Because we often base our self-worth on others' approval and disapproval statements such as, "Well, he wouldn't have done this if I had been a better wife," we often repeatedly take responsibility for others' behavior that was bad. The thought is there must be something wrong with me that made the person treat me so badly.

As I discovered wholeness through my union with Jesus Christ, I changed my attitude toward others. I learned to say to myself: "I am not the Holy Spirit. I am not responsible for another person's behavior. I will not take on their feelings and take on their responsibility. I refuse to ever take ownership for their dysfunctional behavior. And I can't change them, so I won't try to. I will let God be God, and I will do my part."

I'm not saying there are not areas of my life that don't need to be changed and worked on. We must take personal responsibility for the faults that are ours. I personally ask God to show me what needs to be changed in my life, according to His Word. "Show me what areas don't reflect You, God. Let Your Word reflect in me to change me." That is the obligation we all have—to be responsible for our decisions and actions.

I also found through the years that dysfunctional behavior is merely a manifestation of what is happening on the inside of your life. Here's a simple symptom I struggled with years ago: emotional eating. I have made chocolate chip cookies at 3 a.m. on one or more occasions because there was something emotional going on in the inside, and I thought a chocolate chip could at least smooth it out if not solve it. How you feel about yourself will show through in virtually all areas of your life—how you eat, how you walk, how you talk, and how you spend money. It starts from the inside out, not from the outside in. Some areas are more visible and easily identified. I have often said if you see apples all over the ground, you will find a tree nearby.

So How Do We Not Become Codependent?

First, we must have a clear understanding to know what is codependent. This tends to occur when the two first phases of our life—the dependent and independent phases—are not properly developed. It creates a dysfunctional relationship with your self. Your self-worth becomes dependent on external sources. When there is internal conflict of clear identity and worth, it creates dysfunctional relationships externally.

Codependency means we are depending on something outside of ourselves to provide our sense of well-being and direction in life. When you are dependent on others or externals for self-worth and self-definition, you are vulnerable to their inconsistency and conflicts. You give away your power over self-esteem. This is not only dangerous but can be extremely debilitating. When you release your power to others, you position yourself as a victim. A victim mentality says, "I can't get out until you let me out. I can't succeed until you let me succeed." This mentality starts a cycle or pattern that causes us to repeat familiar behaviors reinforcing that belief. So, in turn, we choose untrustworthy people to trust, undependable people to rely upon, and unavailable people to love.

Some of the characteristics of this dynamic include the fear of being alone, the need to be needed, assuming responsibility for others' feelings and behaviors, going from one relationship to the next, and processing an entitlement mentality that thinks people owe us something. When you begin to think like this, you have crippled yourself, because you have limited yourself in life to what they can give you. You demand their love and care and attention, but no one can ever give you enough to satisfy the inner needs of your life. Only God can do that.

Proverbs 3:5–6 tells us to "Trust in the LORD with all your heart, and lean not on your own understanding; in all your ways acknowledge Him, and He shall direct your paths." The word *trust* means to "confide in, so as to be secure and without fear." God says He is the only One who can fully satisfy you and your inner needs. By trusting in God, you find a security that externals can never provide for you. You become "alive," excited about life and eagerly anticipate each day. The most ordinary events and happenings bring a thrill and zest in life, because you find satisfaction from within. You are enthusiastic. Real enthusiasm springs forth from deep inner sources of your spirit.

The word *enthusiasm* is derived from two Greek words, "en" and "theos," meaning "God within you" or "full of God." Therefore, you have a zeal for the gift of life to the extent that God is actively present within you. He is the Giver of life. When you drink of other "wells," trying to satisfy that inner thirst, you find yourself still dehydrated (John 5:4–30). Won't you drink of the living waters today, the wellspring of life, and satisfy the thirst of your soul that is still empty from everything on the outside? When you get full of God, you experience the vitality and effectiveness of life!

Let's review what a healthy interdependent relationship looks like. I am free to be me; you are free to be you. I grow; I change. You grow; you change. Together we are us, and together we grow. As I changed, I became whole and complete, and I could take on the role of being a complement in a healthy relationship.

CHAPTER FOUR

A Closer Look *at* Dysfunction

There are defining moments that caused you and me to become the people we are and to do what we do today. In order to find your way into healthy relationships, you must first come to understand how sick or unhealthy your relationships have been from the past or currently are. Here's why. Sometimes your sickness or dysfunction gets so familiar to you that you think it's normal.

Take a close examination of your relationships with a realistic "audit" in order to make the proper adjustments and changes. When something is not functioning or working properly, it does not mean the whole thing is "faulty." It may just need a part replaced, an addition, or a removal. Your relationships can be similar. You are not "faulty," but perhaps you have not been given the tools needed to build a whole, loving, and respectful relationship. Identify the "part" that is not working and start repairing and building by taking action.

My father committed suicide when I was five years old. The next thirtteen years became a search, a desperate journey, during which I continued to seek in a thousand different ways for the love I longed for from the loss of my father. I know what it is like to feel abandoned, cast aside, and unloved.

One terrible day when I was six years old, my childlike, little figure was sexually and physically abused. Until I was thirteen, it would happen on different occasions and by various people. At a tender young age I had a confused sexual mentality. I thought having sex and connecting with a man in this twisted way became some sort of an affection and emotional attachment. As depraved and perverted as that was, it became normal to me.

Until I realized and understood that it was "sick," I didn't know what healthy was, because unhealthy was my norm. That was why I did what I did and kept perpetuating the dysfunctional behavior until God showed me through His Word that He had a better future for me than my past. I was not a "product" of past experiences or my environment, but I was child of God. I could make active choices as an adult to guide my mind, emotions and soul toward that which is good and true. I had to recognize that I was no longer passively led, or controlled, as a child. I had to take action to determine a new direction for my life. To access your ability to make choices, it's imperative that you chose to be your own person.

I had an experience with Jesus Christ that changed my life and altered me on my personal road to Damascus and transformed me from a Saul to a Paul (Acts 9). The Word of God shone the light of God's truth into my life by revealing the way I had been living was less than the life He had for me. His Word showed me how to get out of that sick situation and break familiar patterns and cycles and understand what real love looks like, what real healing looks like, what real life looks like.

> "The best relationship is the one in which your love for each other exceeds your need for each other."
> —UNKNOWN

The greatest moment of my life was when I accepted Jesus Christ, the living Son of God, as my personal Lord and Savior. I knew I was different. There was a drastic change in my life.

I don't have adequate words to express the dynamics

of what happened when I was shown the plan of God for my life and discovered that God had loved me with an everlasting, undefined, unconditional, pure love. When I came into relationship with God through His Son Jesus, my "empty love tank" was immediately filled. It sounds somewhat "corny," but suddenly the sky was blue, the grass was green, and everything looked different. I suppose that is why the great composer of the famous hymn "Amazing Grace" wrote, "I once was blind, but now I see."

I was rescued. Most of all, *I was loved*. This was the foundation to build a life that God had designed for me. "I know what I'm doing. I have it all planned out—plans to take care of you, not abandon you, plans to give you the future you hope for" (Jeremiah 29:11 THE MESSAGE). And God has given me an amazingly abundant life of grace and forgiveness beyond what I could have imagined. He has the same for you. It is a process of renewing your mind every day by His Word (Romans 12:2) so you can discover and implement that abundant life. It never stops either. Every day you grow and mature as you receive His Word in your life.

To understand what healthy is we have to see our sickness and why we do what we do. It's vital to recount the inconsistent messages from our childhood, because they are the messages being replayed in our life today. You have to ask yourself, what went wrong? Where did it break down? Where did it become dysfunctional?

It's possible that your dysfunction began generations back in your family and that you now find yourself repeating the same cycles. But I am going to give you the steps of how to break free and be liberated from anything that wants to put you into bondage. God has too good of a life for you to continue in that sick cycle.

Here is the critical bridge from a sick past to a healthy future: *to change your life, you have to change the message.* The apostle Paul said, "I beseech you therefore, brethren, by the mercies of God, that you present your bodies a living sacrifice, holy, acceptable to God, which is your reasonable service. And do not be conformed to this world, but be transformed by the renewing of your mind, that you may prove what is that good and acceptable and perfect will of God" (Romans 12:1–2).

The only way I am going to walk out the will of God in my life is to get a renovated mind. I must change the message to change my life. That's why Ephesians 4:23 says, "And be renewed in the spirit of your mind."

But in order for you to change the message, you must be acutely aware of the message. You must have an awareness of what it was that went wrong in your childhood that affects your dysfunction today.

Powerful Messages That Lead to Dysfunction

Let's examine some powerful messages that lead to dysfunction and contribute to the chaos in your life today. You need to identify the message that has affected your life, because you cannot conquer what you don't confront, and you can't confront what you don't identify. The knowledge of how your current thought and behavioral patterns were formed will begin to release you from self-critical indictments that create these sick cycles. Deep embedded messages have to be identified and dealt with.

> "Anger repressed can poison a relationship as surely as the cruelest words."
> —JOYCE BROTHERS

"I Love You, but Go Away. Leave Me Alone."

In some homes the parents are warm and loving, and other times they are angry and rejecting. There is calm and kindness one moment, but throwing the table over the next moment. And the child never knows what he or she is going to get. There is no stability or predictability. The only constant in that child's life is inconsistency. It is like walking through a field of landmines. You never know if the next step is going to be explosive or safe.

If you grew up in this type of home, it explains why you are attracted to the type of person who is warm and loving one day and rejecting and hostile the next day. You play through the role of your childhood over and over again, because the only consistency you know is inconsistency. You are comfortable with chaos but not with stability. Whether you realize it or not, you are so used to not knowing what is coming tomorrow that if everything in your life is peaceful and stable, you will often create chaos because it feels more comfortable and familiar to you. And if a relationship is working well, you will tend to break it, because subconsciously you are unfamiliar with the stability, and therefore you begin to create chaos. You were given mixed messages and never knew what would set your parent off. You can thrive in crisis because it is what you are accustomed to.

In your life, the message "I love you" is inconsistent, so how you deal with all these inconsistencies not only makes you unpredictable but causes you to attract unpredictability.

"You Can Never Do Anything Right, but I Need and Want You."

If you grew up with this message, you could never live up to the standards that were set for you. Never. You never cleaned the dishes good enough. You never made the bed right. You didn't iron the clothes correctly. If you got a B on a test, you were asked why it wasn't an A. When you had a chance to get the game-winning hit, but didn't, you failed. "Why aren't you as good as your older sister?" "Why couldn't you be as smart as your younger brother?"

Whatever the standards were, you could never quite meet them. And if you did meet it, the standard was changed. Your life became a continual performance for acceptance.

If I do this, I'll be loved.

If I make this, I'll be valued.

If I can bring this home, I will be honored and respected.

And you truly believed everything that went wrong was your fault because you were *never quite good enough*.

At the same time, you knew your parent or parents could not get along without you. And since it was impossible for them to make it without you, you would struggle to fix things even though you felt so worthless. You became "The Placater." You become the person who easily and automatically steps into the role of the codependent one in relationships—the enabler who perpetuates the sick cycle.

If you watch whom you are drawn to, you find yourself drawn to people who are extremely dependent on you, but you are never good enough for them. In the Introduction, this was Jill's problem as she related to Charley. You find yourself with people who are highly critical of you, who always put you down, and yet you know they can't live without you. They will always point out your faults, but for the sake of the relationship you find a way to make everything okay. If someone is going to be at fault, it's going to be you. You will always be the scapegoat.

In the Old Testament, the scapegoat or "the goat for Azazel" was the name given to the goat that was taken away into the wilderness on the Day of Atonement (Leviticus 16:8–26). The priest made atonement over the scapegoat, placing the blood of all the sins of Israel on it, and then the goat would be sent away, bearing Israel's guilt to a "land not inhabited."

Is that how you feel? Since you were a child, you carry all the weight of others' criticism, because if there is something wrong, it must be your fault. You take responsibility for others' actions and feelings. When you were treated in a lousy way as a child, you analyzed the situation and concluded you must have either done something wrong or not good enough; therefore, you did not and do not let yourself experience valid emotions. You don't get angry, even though it is a normal and healthy reaction to being treated badly. The Bible says to be angry but sin not (Ephesians 4:26). To not be angry at being mistreated is abnormal and sick.

If you do not adequately know how or are too weak to identify and then give appropriate voice to your emotions, your relationships will be impaired if not doomed.

Feelings, regardless of being "right" or "wrong," have ownership. They belong to us and are valid to the person who possesses them. You have a right to ask for things you need in your relationship. In fact, you have a responsibility to yourself and those you have a relationship with to be clear about your needs.

The message of "You can never do anything right, but I want and need you" will lead you to become so desperately concerned about a loss of control that you give up your feelings and grow up to become the perfect doormat for inconsiderate people. When you don't deal with those valid feelings God gave you—if you keep them repressed—it can and often will push you into depression. If you suppress anger and resentment and stuff it down inside, it will take you into depression and other unhealthy outlets of expression.

"I'll Be There for You the Next Time, I Promise. I Give You My Word."

Children who grow up with this message learn how to not want or express their desire so they don't get disappointed. Afterall, your greatest disappointment comes from your highest expectation. If this was your experience, it will cause you to be tired and resentful, feeling that you do everything in the relationship because it is nearly impossible for you to ever ask for something yourself. And the reason you don't ask is because you are afraid of the disappointment. You expect people to let you down, not follow through with their commitments and even betray you.

Instead of having normal expectations and desires, you don't want to be hurt, so you give up your expectations. And, to survive, you assume people somehow know your needs and will just meet them.

One of the problems with this is that you will never be happy unless you partner up with a mind reader or someone who knows something about your future.

Here's the sick cycle you find yourself trapped in. You fear the rejection and disappointment of asking for something and not getting it, so you don't ask. Beyond that, you also fear that if you do ask you might get it, because you don't know how to receive something. Why is that? Because your fear of disappointment has set you up so much to not have expectations that you can't receive anything. It can be as simple as a compliment. Someone says to you, "You look lovely today," and you shake your head, touch the arm of your sweater, and respond, "Oh, this ugly old thing." It makes you feel weird to receive anything, even a compliment.

> "Assumptions are the termites of relationships."
> —HENRY WINKLER

And so what begins to happen is that you feel other people ought to know what you want and act upon it. But people are not mind readers. They don't know what you want unless you can effectively communicate it to them.

> "Men are from earth. Women are from earth. Deal with it."
> —UNKNOWN

Affective is the key word to expressing your feelings, needs, and desires. *Affective* means emotional. The first step in expressing your feelings and needs is to choose the key word that accurately describes your emotional state. Remember that your feelings often have many layers, which is why I say the "key" word or words. Be able to define what it means to you and to explain the intensity of your feelings—the impact, duration, and context—to help others understand precisely how you feel. Choose your words wisely, accurately, and carefully so that you describe the context of your needs, desires, and feelings without putting others on the defensive or placing blame.

By not doing this, you give up your expectations. Giving up your expectations for having your needs met can lead to bitterness, resentfulness, and only increasing unhappiness.

"Everything Is Fine. Don't Worry. But How Can I Handle All of This?"

Perhaps as a child the message you got over and over was "everything is okay," while the clear underlying sense was that something was wrong. You heard, "It's okay, it's okay. Everything is fine," but when you hadn't had consistent meals in a couple of days, and the lights were turned off, you started to wonder. "It's okay, it's okay," but your parent has not been home in several weeks or called to find out how everything was going.

You get constant mixed messages. Your intuition tells you it is not the way it's being stated. Nothing adds up to "it's okay." And the result is that you develop into a super person by the time you are an adult, because at some moment you decide that you can and you will take charge. You must be the responsible one. Somewhere along the way you decide that "I will take charge, and everything will be okay, no matter what it costs me."

The problem with this position is that Superman or Superwoman does not exist in real life. Super heroes only live in fantasyland. You're human. You are not invincible. Such was the case with Dorcas in Acts 9:36–43. She continued to do more than she was capable of doing, and she ultimately died because she gave out more than she took in. People such as Dorcas give and give and give but don't replenish what is lacking, and end up paying a price. She was doing a good thing, but at an "expense" no one can afford. While helping others is an honorable characteristic, there is a place that crosses over to an unbalanced lifestyle.

The truth is we need to be replenished and renewed.

"But those who wait on the LORD shall renew their strength; they shall mount up with wings like eagles, they shall run and not be weary, they shall walk and not faint" (Isaiah 40:31). We all must be replenished. By resting in God, your weaknesses are made strong, and He enables you to accomplish what you are responsible for. On our own, none of us are capable of doing all things. Remember, there is only one God. Do not try to play God in life. You are human—He is God. Let Him be in control, and simply live the surrendered life of yielding yourself to Him to supply all your needs.

These dysfunctional messages along with many others play out in our life today and create myths rather than truths. Once we have taken a good hard look at the myth, at the message that is inaccurate and still producing the behavior in your life that is creating the sick cycle, it is time to take action and break the pattern.

How Damage Affects Women and Men in Relationships

I have established that if I am going to love you, I have to first love myself. And for me to love myself, I have to understand the love God has for me. How this works out in relationships, though, may not be what you expect. We must take a closer look at the differences between a man and a woman, because it impacts how the damage affects them in relationships.

Adam, according to Genesis 2:15, was created by God and immediately given a job to do. Before Adam had a wife and children, he had a job to fulfill and responsibilities. Adam was birthed into a position and productivity, and the same is true for all men. Men are fulfilled through achievement, career, and position. Men find their worth and value in what they do. If you ask a man, "Who are you?" he will usually describe himself in words that define what he does. "I am a basketball player." "I am a carpenter." "I am an attorney." They describe themselves by their position, by what they do. That's why when a man loses his job or career or when what he does is attacked and damaged, it affects him tremendously. He grapples to find his significance and identity.

Eve is totally different from Adam. God said to Eve, "Your desire shall be for your husband" (Genesis 3:16). While Adam was created from the dust by the hand of God and given a job, woman was created by God from the side of man (Genesis 2:20–22). She was birthed into relationship and positioned next to him to be "a helpmeet." So when you ask a woman, "Who are you?" she will usually describe herself in terms of her relationship connections. "I am the wife of James." "I am the mother of Lily." "I am the daughter of Henry and Betty." "I work for Sheronne." Even a woman who is task-oriented is motivated by the ability to connect relationally when she gets the job done. A woman, in contrast to a man, is hurt when her relationships are attacked and damaged.

Women are relation/nurture-oriented, and men are production/position-oriented. This doesn't mean men aren't nurturers, or they don't need nurturing or care. But it does mean men are affected differently than women. For instance, when a man is considering a job, he wants to cut to the bottom line, clearly define his responsibilities, and find out how much he is going to be paid. For a woman seeking the same job, it's not that money isn't important to her, but she will be more inclined to find her reward in relations at work than the pay, and she will evaluate the work environment accordingly.

It is said that a woman needs a minimum of thirteen touches a day just to survive emotionally. A woman will speak an average of twenty-five to fifty thousand words per day in comparison to a man's mere fifteen to twenty-five thousand words. Women need someone to touch and talk to them to develop a healthy self-esteem.

Because of our fundamental differences, our expressions also vary. Women tend to be emotionally stimulated, while men are sight stimulated. Men are hunters. They see and conquer. Women, being emotional, need to feel. That is why when a man and woman come together intimately, a man is stimulated by what he sees, while a woman is stimulated by how she feels. That's the way God created us.

As men and women, it is crucial that we understand these differences. For instance, I have seen many women struggle to compete for the attention their husband gives to his job. This is damaging to their relationship, and it's not necessary. The husband needs his career position just as much as his wife needs him. When she begins to appreciate and respect his responsibility to fulfill the desire put in him by God to be the provider and worker, he is more likely to emotionally connect with her, providing the nurturing she needs.

Since the Fall, we no longer have the know-how to fulfill our roles perfectly. For instance, the instinct and desire of women to give and receive love is there, but the know-how must be developed. Many times this takes place based on what we have seen or experienced, which is often dysfunctional. As a result, we pattern and carry out behavior that will produce damage in all our relationships, including our relationship with God.

Many men find themselves in the sick cycle of pouring too much of their life into their work. Typically, this happens because there is a void in their life that they are trying to fulfill by the one source from which they get their most productivity and profit and reward. And it is based on what the men have seen or not seen in their role models. If men don't have healthy father role models, then they often won't know how to function fully in relationships. Their children will adopt this same damaged and distorted view and fail to know what healthy is. You won't function in a healthy manner if you don't know what it looks like.

The same sick cycles take place for women as they desire to make healthy relationships function fully. We often don't have the know-how to be developed and to be operational in these relationships. We fail to understand that how we relate to those around us affects how we relate to God. And how we relate to God affects how we relate to ourselves. Or that how we relate to ourselves affects how we relate to those around us. It is a cycle of behavior that is created in our life, which can only be changed through changing our beliefs.

> "You can kiss your family and friends good-bye and put miles between you, but at the same time you carry them with you in your heart, your mind, your stomach, because you do not just live in a world but a world lives in you."
> —FREDERICK BUECHNER

We must get rid of any notions that God deals with us in the same way that some men and women do. God doesn't abandon you. He doesn't abuse or hurt or misuse you. He's not going to do anything wrong or bad to you. He's not "after you." When someone has been violated or messed up by a person, it's hard to understand the meaning of crying out to God as our "Abba, Father" or "Daddy." How do you crawl up in the lap of a Father God when the only model you've ever known would never allow you on his lap? When you did not receive the guarding, governing, or guidance of a natural father, it is difficult to comprehend and receive this from your heavenly Father. If you did not experience the proper bonding process in your early years you could not depend on your parents taking care of your needs in a consistent manner. You couldn't depend on being held, heard and loved to solve your fears, meet your needs and calm your hurts. Therefore, it is difficult to trust that God will actually do that for you.

For years, I had the hardest time when anybody would preach or teach on the theme of "Abba, Father." After my father died when I was a child, whenever I crawled in another male's lap, he wanted sexual favors. How could I cry out, "Abba, Father," when my thinking was so distorted toward any male or father figure? For me it took years of studying the Word, changing my beliefs, casting down imaginations, taking out the old lies, and putting in the truth before I comprehended that God is not like the men who abused me. I can crawl up in His lap, and He will wrap His arms of love around me. He will never hurt me. He doesn't have any wrong motives. He will never leave or forsake me. He doesn't have a back door or a trap door or booby trap.

> God is safe.
> God is secure.
> God is a rock.
> God is a refuge.
> God is a friend.
> God is a strong tower to whom I can run.
> God is my Savior.

God knows how to hold me.

God knows how to take care of me.

God knows how to caress me.

God knows what I need when nobody else understands me.

God created me and loves me unconditionally.

God is always loving, gentle, and kind.

God will protect me.

God will provide for every need I have.

God knows how to counsel and comfort me.

God will never fail me.

I can trust God. He's an awesome God!

CHAPTER FIVE

Where Are Your Scars?

We've all got scars. Words that were said to us when we were young. Things we experienced that we should not have experienced. Things we saw that we should never have seen. As well as lifelong consequences caused from stupid decisions, whether our own or someone else's. I've already told you about some of my own scars. Scars brought about by the wounds of dysfunction in my own family when I was growing up. And there certainly were others too. But the day came when I met Jesus Christ and made other choices and that is when everything in my life changed. So what is my point? Simply this, in order to move forward and live the life that God truly has for you, it's important that you make sure that they are SCARS and not open WOUNDS.

If you keep finding that you are sensitive about certain things, held back by the same unreasonable fears, or that you keep making the same bad decisions over and over again, or that you have habits you just can't quit. No matter what it is, chances are good that you have a wound that never healed right. It's not a scar, it's a wound, or worse yet, an infection and you need to get rid of it and allow God to heal you. Otherwise you will never be in a position to experience the love and relationships you deserve.

My advice to you is to get it cleaned out and get it healed. If that means you need to get some professional help, to talk to a trusted friend about it, or whatever, then do it. The only person that can make the decision to get that part of your life healed is you. A scar is a reminder you've been through the healing process and you have healed. Make no mistake about it scars are a part of life. You cannot acquire wisdom without getting scarred at some point in the process. It's the price we all pay for discovering why what is right, 'is right'. An overly sensitive attitude, a lingering destructive habit, a fearful mindset just shows us that we have wounds we need to work on.

Throughout scripture we are given example after

example of people who became victorious in their lives and in each and every case they were victims of dysfunctional relationships that had wounded them and left them scarred. No exceptions. Yes, they had been wounded and yes, they had healed, and yes, they were left scarred. BUT the point is they had healed and the scars were only reminders of what they had overcome. The same is true for you and me and everyone else that has ever lived. Let me give you a few examples.

Do you remember the story of Jacob? Jacob was the grandson of Abraham and the second son of Abraham's son Isaac. Though he was a twin to his brother Esau, Jacob was still the second born of the two sons and as a result his brother Esau was to receive the birthright and all the blessings that went with it. That was how society functioned at the time.

Through no fault of his own, Jacob was relegated to second place and no matter what he did he could not win the love or approval of his father. What do you think that did to Jacob? How do think it made him feel about himself? I'll tell you how it made him feel. He felt like many of us feel that have felt relegated to second place. It left a festering wound that caused him to do all kinds of things to win approval that he probably would not have done if dad had been a little more fair and attentive.

As a result Jacob played by his own rules and tricked Esau out of both his birthright and his father's blessing. Ultimately the wounds became so deep and the rift so far between both Jacob and Esau that they hated each other to the point that Esau was going to kill Jacob. What happened next? Jacob ran for his life. Yet, in the process he meets God, and learns all the life lessons caused by his own deceit on the way to becoming the man of God that he ultimately became.

Does that mean Jacob quit making mistakes? Are you kidding? He was very human. He even made the mistake of taking on the Angel of the Lord in an all night wrestling match. Granted, he limped the rest of his life because of it but that's beside the point. He was human, he made mistakes and continued to make mistakes throughout his life and yet God loved him and blessed him in spite of it. He even became the patriarch of the nation of Israel.

In spite of the fact, that Jacob knew first hand the sting of personal rejection the Bible tells us that Jacob does it himself to his wife Leah and later to ten of his own sons. It isn't something he does intentionally or maliciously, he seems to be oblivious to it and yet it all works into the biblical narrative to a positive ending through the power of God.

In Genesis 29, it says that no matter what his wife Leah does to win his love and affection, Jacob's affection is for Leah's sister, Rachel. Leah feels unloved. Granted, Jacob wanted Rachel all along and it is true that Leah was used as a pawn in a chess match between her father Laban and Jacob but can you imagine how Leah must have felt? You can't help but pity her. In fact, it says that God pitied her and opened her womb so that she could give Jacob children while Rachel was barren. In all, Leah gave Jacob six sons, Reuben, Simeon, Levi, Judah, Issachar and Zebulon as well as a daughter, Dinah. Yet, the word of God says Leah never felt loved by Jacob. So was this all a mistake? Absolutely not! Don't forget that one day the Messiah, Jesus Christ would be born through the line of Judah, one of the sons that Leah gave birth to. But still, was Leah wounded by rejection? Did she have scars? You know she did.

It's during the time that Leah is having her children that Rachel becomes very jealous of her sister and insists that Jacob give her children through her handmaiden Bilhah. Bilhah then gives birth to two sons. First Dan and then sometime later Naphtali. Leah then decides to give Jacob her handmaiden Zilpah, and Zilpah gives Jacob two sons Gad and Asher. At this point in the story Jacob has ten sons.

The word then goes on to tell us in Genesis 30 that after many years had passed that God opened Rachel's womb and she gave birth to a son and named him Joseph. She later died giving birth to Joseph's brother Benjamin (Genesis 35) and was buried at Bethlehem.

There is a reason I am giving you this background. It's because I want you to understand that because we live in a fallen world, *dysfunction* is the norm and not the exception even in the lives of the greatest people in scripture. It is recorded in the Bible so that we can see the mistakes others have made and guard against making the same mistakes in our own lives.

From the very beginning the sons born to Leah could clearly see that their father showed love and affection for Rachel that they did not see him giving their mother, Leah. Then when Rachel gave birth to Joseph, it became immediately obvious that dad had a favorite. It was Joseph, the son he had through Rachel. This is where the story gets really interesting. We are told Genesis 37:3-4:

³ "Jacob loved Joseph more than any of his other children because Joseph had been born to him in his old age. So one day Jacob had a special gift made for Joseph—a beautiful robe.⁴ But his brothers hated Joseph because their father loved him more than the rest of them. They couldn't say a kind word to him."

It was right after this that we are told that Joseph who was all of 17 years of age at the time had a dream, a dream that he shares with his half brothers. He tells them that he dreamt they would all being bowing to him as is recorded in Genesis 37: 6-11:

⁶ He said to them, "Listen to this dream I had: ⁷ We were binding sheaves of grain out in the field when suddenly my sheaf rose and stood upright, while your sheaves gathered around mine and bowed down to it."

⁸ His brothers said to him, "Do you intend to reign over us? Will you actually rule us?" And they hated him all the more because of his dream and what he had said.

⁹ Then he had another dream, and he told it to his brothers. "Listen," he said, "I had another dream, and this time the sun and moon and eleven stars were bowing down to me."

¹⁰ When he told his father as well as his brothers, his father rebuked him and said, "What is this dream you had? Will your mother and I and your brothers actually come and bow down to the ground before you?" ¹¹ His brothers were jealous of him, but his father kept the matter in mind.

Needless to say, they were outraged. They already hated him for being dad's favorite but now he was telling them that he would one day rule over them as well and from that point on they were looking for a way to either kill him or get rid of him.

Now lets stop and reassess. OK, it isn't Joseph's fault that he was born to Rachel instead of Leah. And it isn't his fault that dad dotes on him in preference to of any of his other sons. But jealousy and envy took root and what follows is an amazing story of how in spite of experiencing the worst kind of hardship and betrayal God can work through the most difficult of circumstances to bring about reconciliation and forgiveness and even an understanding that God truly is in control of our lives even when we are not aware of it.

In the next part of the story Joseph's ten brothers are grazing their flocks of sheep at a place called Shechem. Dad is wondering how his sons are doing so he sends Joseph to visit them and to bring word back to him about how things are going. In Genesis 37:14 it states, *¹⁴ So he said to him, "Go and see if all is well with your brothers and with the flocks, and bring word back to me." Then he sent him off from the Valley of Hebron.* When Joseph got to Shechem he couldn't find them but a man that saw him wandering the fields asked him what he was looking for and when he told the man that he was looking for his brothers the man said, "I heard them say they were going to Dothan." So Joseph was on his way to Dothan.

When his brothers saw him at a distance, they thought, 'Now is our chance to get rid of that dreamer once and for all.' They discussed how they would kill him, throw his body into a cistern, and then tell their father that a ferocious animal had eaten him. At this point Joseph's oldest brother Reuben intervenes and convinces the others not to kill him or to shed blood but to throw him into an empty cistern that had no water in it. It was Reuben's idea to come back later and to pull him out and send him home. So they stripped him of his beautiful robe and threw him into the cistern.

A short time later as his brothers were discussing what to do him, they saw a caravan of Ishmaelite traders from Midian on their way to Egypt. His brother Judah said, "There's no point in killing him. After all, like it or not, he is our brother so lets sell him to the Midianites." They all agreed. So Joseph was sold for twenty pieces of silver to the Midianites. Then they took his ornate robe and covered it with blood from a freshly killed goat and went to see their father with it and asked him, "Is this your sons robe?" Naturally, Jacob was devastated. He believed that some wild animal had eaten his son Joseph, and that it was his fault for having sent him. It was a heartache that Jacob was never to get over. He never stopped mourning.

But Joseph wasn't dead. He was taken by the Midianites traders into the land of Egypt and there he was resold. This time to Potiphar, the Captain of the Kings Guard. In Genesis 39:2-6 we then read:

> ² *The* LORD *was with Joseph, so he succeeded in everything he did as he served in the home of his Egyptian master.* ³ *Potiphar noticed this and realized that the* LORD *was with Joseph, giving him success in everything he did.* ⁴ *This pleased Potiphar, so he soon made Joseph his personal attendant. He put him in charge of his entire household and everything he owned.* ⁵ *From the day Joseph was put in charge of his master's household and property, the* LORD *began to bless Potiphar's household for Joseph's sake. All his household affairs ran smoothly, and his crops and livestock flourished.* ⁶ *So Potiphar gave Joseph complete administrative responsibility over everything he owned. With Joseph there, he didn't worry about a thing—except what kind of food to eat!*

Can you imagine what Joseph must have felt at this point to have fully realized that his own brothers had actually wanted to kill him but instead had sold him into slavery? Yet, I'm sure that in some ways it was not lost on Joseph that he was actually very fortunate because here he was probably living pretty much in the lap of luxury and held in very high regard by his master.

Unfortunately, trouble was brewing. In Verse 7 of the same chapter it states: *Joseph was a very handsome and well-built young man, ⁷ and Potiphar's wife soon began to look at him lustfully. "Come and sleep with me," she demanded.* In truth, this is one time that the scripture may actually be understating. Why do I say that? Because if you were to read, *'Antiquities of the Jews'* by Jewish Historian Flavius Josephus, Book Two, chapter four, you would read this about Joseph: *"For when his master's wife was fallen in love with him, both on account of his beauty of body, and his dexterous management of affairs; and supposed that if she should make it known to him, she should easily persuade him to come and lie with her..."* Josephus then goes on to say that not only would Joseph not take advantage of the situation but he also says the following about Joseph when he was falsely accused of trying to rape her. *"Now Joseph, commending all his affairs to God, did not betake himself to make his defense, nor to give an account of the circumstances of the fact: but silently underwent the bonds and the distress he was in. Firmly believing, that God, who knew the cause of his affliction, and the truth of the fact, would be more powerful than those that inflicted the punishments upon him. A proof of whose providence he quickly received: for the keeper of the prison taking notice of his care and fidelity in the affairs he had set him about, and the dignity of his countenance, relaxed his bonds; and thereby made his heavy calamity lighter and more supportable to him. He also permitted him to make use of a diet better than that of the rest of the prisoners."*

Now consider this, if you were Joseph what would you think? How would you feel if you went from living in the lap of luxury to being sent to prison for a crime you never committed because you were unwilling to go against your conscience and instead you do the right thing because it's the right thing? Do you think he thought it was unfair? Of course he did but Joseph had a *relationship* with his God. He trusted God.

The scripture says that he while he was in prison he met two different men that had both been personal attendants to the King. One was the King's Cup Bearer and the other his personal baker. Both men had dreams and Joseph accurately interpreted the meaning of each man's dream. To the Cup Bearer he stated, "You will be restored to your former position in three days time. Remember me, sir, when you are restored." In three days time the man was in fact restored but the Bible says he forgot about Joseph completely until an event two years later.

Two years later, the King (Pharaoh) has dreams, nightmares actually, that frighten him. He has an ominous feeling about the dream and he wants to know what the dreams mean but no one can interpret them. It is then that the King's Cup Bearer remembers Joseph as stated in Genesis 41:9-13, *"9 Finally, the king's chief cup-bearer spoke up. "Today I have been reminded of my failure,"* he told Pharaoh. *10 "Some time ago, you were angry* with the chief baker and me, and you imprisoned us in the palace of the captain of the guard. ¹¹ One night the chief baker and I each had a dream, and each dream had its own meaning. ¹² There was a young Hebrew man with us in the prison who was a slave of the captain of the guard. We told him our dreams, and he told us what each of our dreams meant. ¹³ And everything happened just as he had predicted. I was restored to my position as cup-bearer, and the chief baker was executed and impaled on a pole."

Pharaoh immediately ordered for Joseph to be brought to him from prison. The Bible says that he was shaved, that means the hair on his head, his beard, his chest, everything, because the Egyptians were meticulous about cleanliness. Then he was given new clothes and brought before the King. We are then told in verses 15 through 36 of the same chapter the following:

¹⁵ Then Pharaoh said to Joseph, "I had a dream last night, and no one here can tell me what it means. But I have heard that when you hear about a dream you can interpret it."

¹⁶ "It is beyond my power to do this," Joseph replied. "But God can tell you what it means and set you at ease."

¹⁷ So Pharaoh told Joseph his dream. "In my dream," he said, "I was standing on the bank of the Nile River, ¹⁸ and I saw seven fat, healthy cows come up out of the river and begin grazing in the marsh grass. ¹⁹ But then I saw seven sick-looking cows, scrawny and thin, come up after them. I've never seen such sorry-looking animals in all the land of

Egypt. ²⁰ These thin, scrawny cows ate the seven fat cows. ²¹ But afterward you wouldn't have known it, for they were still as thin and scrawny as before! Then I woke up.

²² "In my dream I also saw seven heads of grain, full and beautiful, growing on a single stalk. ²³ Then seven more heads of grain appeared, but these were blighted, shriveled, and withered by the east wind. ²⁴ And the shriveled heads swallowed the seven healthy heads. I told these dreams to the magicians, but no one could tell me what they mean."

²⁵ Joseph responded, "Both of Pharaoh's dreams mean the same thing. God is telling Pharaoh in advance what he is about to do. ²⁶ The seven healthy cows and the seven healthy heads of grain both represent seven years of prosperity. ²⁷ The seven thin, scrawny cows that came up later and the seven thin heads of grain, withered by the east wind, represent seven years of famine.

²⁸ "This will happen just as I have described it, for God has revealed to Pharaoh in advance what he is about to do. ²⁹ The next seven years will be a period of great prosperity throughout the land of Egypt. ³⁰ But afterward there will be seven years of famine so great that all the prosperity will

> **"You must begin to trust yourself. If you do not, then you will forever be looking to others to prove your own merit to you, and you will never be satisfied. You will always be asking others what to do and at the same time resenting those from whom you seek such aid."**
> —UNKNOWN

be forgotten in Egypt. Famine will destroy the land. ³¹ This famine will be so severe that even the memory of the good years will be erased. ³² As for having two similar dreams, it means that these events have been decreed by God, and he will soon make them happen.

³³ "Therefore, Pharaoh should find an intelligent and wise man and put him in charge of the entire land of Egypt. ³⁴ Then Pharaoh should appoint supervisors over the land and let them collect one-fifth of all the crops during the seven good years. ³⁵ Have them gather all the food produced in the good years that are just ahead and bring it to Pharaoh's storehouses. Store it away, and guard it so there will be food in the cities. ³⁶ That way there will be enough to eat when the seven years of famine come to the land of Egypt. Otherwise this famine will destroy the land."

The Bible says the King and his officials, not only believed Joseph's interpretation of the King's dream but they immediately had a meeting to discuss what to do. We'll pick up now in verse 38:

³⁸ So Pharaoh asked his officials, "Can we find anyone else like this man so obviously filled with the spirit of God?" ³⁹ Then Pharaoh said to Joseph, "Since God has revealed the meaning of the dreams to you, clearly no one else is as intelligent or wise as you are. ⁴⁰ You will be in charge of my court, and all my people will take orders from you. Only I, sitting on my throne, will have a rank higher than yours."

⁴¹ Pharaoh said to Joseph, "I hereby put you in charge of the entire land of Egypt." ⁴² Then Pharaoh removed his

signet ring from his hand and placed it on Joseph's finger. He dressed him in fine linen clothing and hung a gold chain around his neck. ⁴³ Then he had Joseph ride in the chariot reserved for his second-in-command. And wherever Joseph went, the command was shouted, "Kneel down!" So Pharaoh put Joseph in charge of all Egypt. ⁴⁴ And Pharaoh said to him, "I am Pharaoh, but no one will lift a hand or foot in the entire land of Egypt without your approval."

⁴⁵ Then Pharaoh gave Joseph a new Egyptian name, Zaphenath-paneah. He also gave him a wife, whose name was Asenath. She was the daughter of Potiphera, the priest of On. So Joseph took charge of the entire land of Egypt. ⁴⁶ He was thirty years old when he began serving in the court of Pharaoh, the king of Egypt. And when Joseph left Pharaoh's presence, he inspected the entire land of Egypt.

⁴⁷ As predicted, for seven years the land produced bumper crops. ⁴⁸ During those years, Joseph gathered all the crops grown in Egypt and stored the grain from the surrounding fields in the cities. ⁴⁹ He piled up huge amounts of grain like sand on the seashore. Finally, he stopped keeping records because there was too much to measure.

⁵⁰ During this time, before the first of the famine years, two sons were born to Joseph and his wife, Asenath, the daughter of Potiphera, the priest of On. ⁵¹ Joseph named his older son Manasseh, for he said, "God has made me forget all my troubles and everyone in my father's family." ⁵² Joseph named his second son Ephraim, for he said, "God has made me fruitful in this land of my grief."

⁵³ *At last the seven years of bumper crops throughout the land of Egypt came to an end.* ⁵⁴ *Then the seven years of famine began, just as Joseph had predicted. The famine also struck all the surrounding countries, but throughout Egypt there was plenty of food.* ⁵⁵ *Eventually, however, the famine spread throughout the land of Egypt as well. And when the people cried out to Pharaoh for food, he told them, "Go to Joseph, and do whatever he tells you."* ⁵⁶ *So with severe famine everywhere, Joseph opened up the storehouses and distributed grain to the Egyptians, for the famine was severe throughout the land of Egypt.* ⁵⁷ *And people from all around came to Egypt to buy grain from Joseph because the famine was severe throughout the world.*

Now I want you to consider the following. The story of Joseph makes it clear that even though life is not always fair God is paying attention. He loves you. He never leaves you. Yes, there may be times that it appears that one bad thing after another just keeps coming our way. I know. I've been there, done that. But let me also tell you, that's the time to dig in closer and closer to God. Think about it. Joseph was hated and betrayed by his own brothers and he did nothing to deserve it. He was sold into slavery but instead of feeling sorry for himself or remaining bitter toward his brothers he made the very best of his situation. He was then accused of a crime he never committed and put in prison for several years. Even then, he made the best of his situation. Yet, through it all, he allowed God to heal him. Did he have wounds? You bet he did. Read verse 51,*"God has made me forget all my troubles and everyone in my father's family."* Did he have scars? How could he not after what his brothers had done or the episode with Potiphar's wife? But in verse 52 he says, *"God has made me fruitful in this land of my grief."* Give this story serious thought. There is no way that Joseph could have awakened one morning while in prison and said to himself, "Wow, before this day is over I'm going to be the number one ruler in the land of Egypt next to the King." It didn't happen like that. He couldn't have known. Yet, throughout the entire thirteen years from the time that he was sold as a slave by his brothers, to the time he was taken from prison and elevated to the highest honor in the land of Egypt at age 30, he was patient and he remained faithful to God. I'm telling you this because I want you to realize that God can turn things around for you if you are diligent, do the best you can in every situation and trust him. Yes, you'll get a few scars along the way but they will only serve as reminders of all that you have experienced and survived.

Obviously, there is a great deal more to the story of Joseph. It gets very intense at times but there is reconciliation and restoration and there are eight key verses that I would like to end this chapter with that really say it all. You'll find them in Genesis 50:14-21:

[14] After burying Jacob, Joseph returned to Egypt with his brothers and all who had accompanied him to his father's burial. [15] But now that their father was dead, Joseph's brothers became fearful. "Now Joseph will show his anger and pay us back for all the wrong we did to him," they said.

¹⁶ So they sent this message to Joseph: "Before your father died, he instructed us ¹⁷ to say to you: 'Please forgive your brothers for the great wrong they did to you—for their sin in treating you so cruelly.' So we, the servants of the God of your father, beg you to forgive our sin." When Joseph received the message, he broke down and wept. ¹⁸ Then his brothers came and threw themselves down before Joseph. "Look, we are your slaves!" they said.

¹⁹ But Joseph replied, "Don't be afraid of me. Am I God, that I can punish you? ²⁰ You intended to harm me, but God intended it all for good. He brought me to this position so I could save the lives of many people. ²¹ No, don't be afraid. I will continue to take care of you and your children." So he reassured them by speaking kindly to them.

By speaking kindly to them Joseph demonstrated God's healing power of forgiveness and restoration that is available to everyone who seeks Him and remains faithful thru life's trials and hardships. Trials and hardships leave scars but our scars are simply a reminder of wounds God has healed.

CHAPTER SIX

Three Steps *to* Breaking *a* Generational Curse

We have seen that dysfunctional messages play out in our life and continue to produce a sick cycle or stronghold of behavior that keeps us from living truly freely. Many are repetitive patterns that plagued our parents or grandparents and were handed down to us as generational curses. It is time to take action and break these pitfalls of addictions, destructive habits, depression, or fear that bind us. (Prov 26:2) Solomon makes it clear that there is always a reason for every curse: "Like a flitting sparrow, like a flying swallow, so a curse without a cause shall not be alight".

Step One
Acknowledge the Inaccurate Message

If you don't acknowledge the inaccurate message in your life, you cannot defeat it.

Leviticus 26:40 is a verse you need to meditate upon: "But if they confess their iniquity and the iniquity of their fathers, with their unfaithfulness in which they were unfaithful to Me, and that they also have walked contrary to Me."

We often think of "iniquity" as an outward sin, such as lying, cheating, getting drunk, or sleeping around. However, the "iniquity" spoken of here is *the perpetual, habitual sins of your forefathers.* For instance, when a father has a sinful lifestyle, his children are likely to have the same sinful lifestyle as well. It might be a violent temper, a sexual addiction, alcoholism, deceitfulness, fearfulness, a drug addiction, and on and on.

It is vital to look at the patterns of behavior of your family history and stop pretending Mommy and Daddy and Granddaddy and Great Grandma were okay if they weren't. By not acknowledging them, we keep ourselves in darkness. The enemy works in darkness.

For true liberation, we must take off the mask of hypocrisy. The word *hypocrite* comes from the Greek theatrical actors who wore a mask of disguise. Freedom starts by having the courage to confront what does not align itself to the promises that God provided in His covenant to us and to not walk in false pretenses any longer. Do not let shame, feelings of guilt, vulnerability, or fear hold you back from being free any longer. The truth is that all have "sinned" or missed the mark. There is not a person who has ever lived who does not struggle with or have some kind of "issue" that has plagued their family.

It's time to have a housecleaning and break the cycle so our children do not perpetuate the sick behavior. God said, "I have set before you life and death, blessing and cursing; therefore choose life, that both you and your descendants may live" (Deuteronomy 30:19). Someone has to break the sick cycle. Someone has to say the buck stops here. Refuse to see your children be messed up or your great grandchildren messed up. It is not only your opportunity to establish a new pattern for your family but also your responsibility.

I made a decision that if I had to work every hour of every day for the rest of my life to see my dysfunction broken, I would do it. I will serve the Lord and get understanding to see my house become a house of wholeness and restoration.

Write this down. "I am only as sick as my secrets."

What plagues most of us is that we are afraid to be real because of what others might think about us. We fear their rejection. Recognize that you don't need acceptance by the ones who would reject you anyway. You have already been accepted by God (Ephesians 1:6). The truth is they probably see the sickness oozing through anyway. Why hide it? It takes way too much energy trying to fake it and cover it up all the time. Recognize that people are pretty much the same. We all have deficiencies in our life. Some have them to a greater degree than others do, but all people have some form of "brokenness". That is part of our human experience.

You can look like the perfect "Holy Church Lady" and praise the Lord just right, but if you're a mess, it's time to get real with yourself. God loves you unconditionally. God gave His Son for you to live an abundant life, so you don't have to compromise and live at a low level. God has a great life for you and a great future, and by hanging on to the junk of your past, you are eliminating the future God has for you. When you stay in this condition, you eliminate walking in the fullness and satisfying relationship God has for you.

As long as you say, "Someday I'm going to get out," you postpone your deliverance. It's time to say, "Come on, God. It's time for You to do whatever You need to do. I will confess the iniquity of my forefathers. It's over."

Take to heart these words: "Then I will remember My covenant with Jacob, and My covenant with Isaac and

My covenant with Abraham I will remember" (Leviticus 26:42). When you acknowledge your dysfunction, your area of vulnerability and weakness, God says He will remember you. Until you admit this is the area of your need, there can never be healing.

Step Two
Reject the Generational Curse

Second Corinthians 10:5 is the key scripture here: "Casting down arguments and every high thing that exalts itself against the knowledge of God, bringing every thought into captivity to the obedience of Christ."

The word *imagination* comes from the Greek word *logismos*, which means "reasoning, thought, or logic." It is the way people think based on their tradition, experience, or past teaching. It is their learned behavior. A *stronghold* is supported by demonic influence. Strongholds do two things: first, they keep people from knowledge and revelation of truth, and, second, they prevent people from walking in obedience. The result of this is ignorance and rebellion—both of which cause you to "perish." Strongholds are also known as "mindsets." A mindset is a fixed and rigid thought process that is resistant to change. The power of a spiritual stronghold is its ability to argue, reason, or influence people to believe they cannot change. You absolutely can change with God on your side. There is nothing impossible or too hard for

God and you, working together.

Until you know who God is in your life, you can't cast anything down. Until you first get into the Word with an awareness of what God has to say, you cannot reject a generational curse or dysfunction. Why? Because the Word of God becomes a mirror and reflection of what you should act like, what you are entitled to, and what you can benefit from. Until I have an awareness of what that Word says by covenant to me, I can never walk it out and execute it in my life.

> If the Word says it, I can be it.
> If the Word says it, I can do it.
> If the Word says it, I can have it.
> If the Word says it, that settles it.

So how can I cast something down unless I know it is contrary to the Word? When I know God's Word says I can live in perfect peace, I can refuse to allow chaos and confusion to rule in my life. I will not stay up all night worrying and fretting and having anxiety attacks over what might happen, because God has said my mind will be in perfect peace. When I know and apply the Word to my life, I begin to see the promised results.

This is not wishful thinking. It is the truth of God, but to make it work requires action on your part. You can't prevent life, but you can reject every message that contradicts the Word of God. People are going to do what they are going to do, but you have the authority to take the Word of God and work the Word in your life. If their actions or words or attitudes are against you, it does not have to detour you from what God says you can have or be. By the power of God's Word, you can reject the dysfunction and take your stand in the truth. Blessings result from hearing Gods voice and doing what He says. Curses result from not hearing Gods voice and not doing what He says.

Step Three
Replace the Broken Generational Curse With the Truth of God's Word

You are aware of the lies that have been passed down from your past, and you have rejected them. You must leave it behind and then cleave to the Word of God. Let the lies and criticism and guilt and dysfunction go, and in its place plant the truth.

If you take these three steps, you will be on your way to freedom.

Here are some vital biblical truths you need to replace the lies you may have had working in your life:

> "*I will praise You, for I am fearfully and wonderfully made; marvelous are Your works, and that my soul knows very well.*" —Psalm 139:14

This is God's fundamental truth over you.
This is what He says about who you are.

This is what you need to say and believe about yourself.

> *"For we are His workmanship, created in Christ Jesus for good works, which God prepared beforehand that we should walk in them."* —EPHESIANS 2:10

You are the product of Almighty God.
You were not an accident or a mistake.
You were purposed and planned in God's heart and mind.

> *"Having predestined us to adoption as sons by Jesus Christ to Himself, according to the good pleasure of His will."* —EPHESIANS 1:5

God is delighted to receive you as His son or daughter.
You need to delight in your position in Jesus Christ.
No matter who rejects you, God accepts you.

> *"But God demonstrates His own love toward us, in that while we were still sinners, Christ died for us."* —ROMANS 5:8

God's love is unconditional.
He loved us when we were unlovable.
He loved us when we were His enemies.

> *"But thanks be to God, who gives us the victory through our Lord Jesus Christ."* —1 CORINTHIANS 15:57

You are victorious in Christ.

You are not striving for victory.

Step into the victory that has already been given to you.

"Who has saved us and called us with a holy calling, not according to our works, but according to His own purpose and grace which was given to us in Christ Jesus before time began." —2 Timothy 1:9

> **"No one can make you feel inferior without your consent."**
> —ELEANOR ROOSEVELT

God loved and chose you in eternity to be His own.

You didn't earn your calling and never will. It's all by His grace.

You did not choose God first. God chose you.

"Yet in all these things we are more than conquerors through Him who loved us." —Romans 8:37

You are more.

You are always more through Christ.

Never let anyone make you less.

"Now then, we are ambassadors for Christ, as though God were pleading through us: we implore you on Christ's behalf, be reconciled to God."
—2 Corinthians 5:20

You have royal blood flowing through your veins.

You are in this world but not of this world.

You are light in the midst of darkness.

"Knowing, beloved brethren, your election by God."
—1 Thessalonians 1:4

You didn't find God. He found you.

You are a chosen generation, a peculiar people, set aside for a purpose.

Gods love undergirds you and you are a part of His family.

The Bible also says:

- A thousand shall fall at your side and ten thousand at your right hand, but destruction will not come near you because you are protected in God (Psalm 91:6–7).
- No weapon formed against you will ever be able to prosper (Isaiah 54:17).
- God orders your footsteps. He's made a path for you, and He's directing your ways (Proverbs 3:6).
- You are hedged in, and you are protected by the blood of Jesus (Job 1:10).
- You are the apple of God's eye (Psalm 17:8).
- You are accepted in the Beloved (Ephesians 1:6).
- You are an heir of God and a joint heir of Jesus Christ (Romans 8:17).
- Blessings shall come upon you and overtake you as you obey the voice of the Lord (Deuteronomy 28:2).
- You are complete and whole in Christ, who is the head of all principality and power (Colossians 2:10).

- God always leads you in triumph in Christ and through you diffuses the fragrance of His knowledge in every place (2 Corinthians 2:14).
- You are rooted and built up in Christ and established in the faith (Colossians 2:7).
- You are the head and not the tail (Deuteronomy 28:13).
- You have favor in the eyes of the Lord (Genesis 6:8).
- You have the mind of Christ (1 Corinthians 2:16).
- You are strong in the Lord and in the power of His might (Ephesians 6:10).
- You are created in God's image and likeness (Genesis 1:26–27).
- You reign in life by Jesus Christ (Romans 5:17).
- You are blessed (2 Corinthians 1:20).
- Your descendants are blessed (Deuteronomy 28:4).
- You are a liberated person by the truth that you know (John 8:32).

To any messages in your life that are less than the truth of God's Word, declare you will not compromise. You will not go back to low-life living. God is calling you to rise up. He may have called you while you were sitting on a barstool. He may have called you while you were lying in a defiled bed. He may have called you when you were as lost as a goose in a winter storm. But His call is by grace to raise you up with Christ and seat you in heavenly realms in Christ Jesus (Eph 2:6)

Remember that when God looked upon the boy

David, He saw a king, and He had David anointed to be king years in advance of David taking on the role (1 Samuel 16). When Gideon was a coward, God called him a great man of valor (Judges 6), because He knew what Gideon could become. Through God, you will break the sick cycle and dysfunction that has plagued your life and held you back.

You may have to end some relationships that are wrong for you or hurting you, but it's worth it. You must choose to not compromise your character for anyone. Decide that you will not be controlled any longer by another person's dysfunction or egocentric mess. You won't give power to any person to manipulate and control you. No person can make you lose your joy, your temper, or any other aspect unless you give that person that power. Don't do it!

You can state: "Sorry, but I am free. I have discovered and been set free by the truth of God's Word, and I will overcome my condition. I will not compromise myself because I now know myself. The labels of the past came through events, but that's not who I am. I am a new person, complete and whole, through Jesus Christ."

CHAPTER SEVEN

A New Start *in* Healthy Relationships

If we carefully consider our relationships, we'll often note that we keep putting ourselves in positions that are almost self-fulfilled prophecies. If we analyze it closely, we will realize we attract what we subconsciously think we deserve.

For instance, a woman gets Mr. 6'2" with blond hair and blue eyes, and he emotionally abuses her. She gets rid of him and goes out to look for a new man. Then she gets Mr. 5'1" with dark hair and dark eyes, and he emotionally abuses her, too. She says, "But they look so different and seemed so different. Why are they doing the same thing?" It's because something subconsciously in her is sending out the signal that that's what she believes she deserves.

So what does she need to do?

Find People Who Value You and Build Upon Mutual Love and Respect

You have to go and find where you are valued. You need to go where you are celebrated, not where you are merely tolerated. Remember the lessons we learned from Leah. Because of her own insecurities, she kept taking the blessings God gave her and using them for the wrong reasons. Leah birthed the blessings of son after son, which God gave her, but she used them for the wrong purpose and reason. She used them to try to win Jacob's love and affection and attention.

Ask yourself whether you are going to waste a lifetime trying to get somebody to like you, love you, and celebrate you, when they don't have enough discernment to see the value or the gifting God has given you. Either that person is just a fool, or God has blinded them from seeing the treasure in you because He knows they will be dangerous to you and your future. When a person doesn't value you, they will eventually violate you in some way.

Remember that the first command God gave Abraham was to get away from his crazy kinfolk (Genesis 12:1). He said to get away from people who don't value you. Get away from people who don't see what God is doing in your life. Cut off the relationships that are toxic. Unfortunately, Abraham allowed Lot to tag along, and Lot became a serious problem to him. The process to moving on to healthy connecting is found in learning to let go.

You have to find people who value you. Don't waste your time trying to force-feed people who are not hungry for the gift that is in you. There are starving people who are desperate for what you possess, so why try to get somebody who is fat and gluttonous and doesn't want to feast from the gift in your life. There is a whole world of other people who hunger and value what God has placed inside of you. Life is too short to waste it on those who devalue you. The landscape of your soul is similar to your house. Your self-destructive patterns and sense of worthlessness take up many rooms. When you let go of the unloving parts that you have tightly held on to before, you make room for an infinite amount of love, respect and acceptance.

> "When men and women are able to respect and accept their differences then love has a chance to blossom."
> —JOHN GRAY

In the parable of the great feast (Luke 14:15–24),

Jesus gives a picture of one man's actions that are similar to what we need to do. He tells about a master who has prepared a wonderful feast and calls all those he's invited to come. The banqueting table was ready and available, but apparently those who were invited weren't hungry. They made a variety of excuses for why they didn't come and eat, which angered the master. So he told his servant to go to "the poor and the maimed and the lame and the blind. . . . Go out into the highways and hedges, and compel them to come in, that my house may be filled" (vv. 21–23). In order words, the master said go find anyone who was hungry for what he'd prepared.

> "It is only when we no longer compulsively need someone that we can have a real relationship with them."
> —ANTHONY STORR

That's what you need to do. Don't stay frustrated by people who do not value and appreciate who you are. If they're not hungry, stop trying to force-feed them what they don't want. Don't allow them to get you to question your validity or wonder what's wrong with you. If you're asking them, "Why don't you love me? Why don't you like me?" you are either with a fool or with somebody whom God has blinded because he or she is not the person with whom God wants you to be in covenant. Remember the nature of love is not force. Evil can be forced on us; love, real love, cannot.

Isn't that what happened with the Samaritan woman

in John 4? She was so thirsty to be valued that she changed men in her life like most of us change clothes. She went from one unfulfilling relationship to the next because she was thirsty. Fortunately for her, one day she encountered Jesus Christ. And Jesus spoke straight to her heart and said, "Hey, listen. You've been drinking from the wrong well. All those wells have left you thirsting, because they don't have the ability to satisfy your true heart's desire. But if you drink of Me, you will never thirst again."

When the Samaritan woman believed Jesus was who He said He was, I can almost hear the gigantic sigh of relief she must have given. After years of searching for the fulfillment to the deepest desires of her life, she had found the Source that could not fail her. No wonder she dropped her water pot and brought others to Jesus. She was transformed!

Most of us have a dysfunctional habit in our life that is similar to the Samaritan woman. We keep going to a well that doesn't have what we need, and we are so thirsty because we're never satisfied. We keep going to another person who doesn't have the Living Water, and we drink contaminated water that is not able to hydrate the thirst of our spirit and soul. That person does not have the capability of giving us what we need and can only receive from God. We put demands on others that cannot be met by them. When we drink of the Living Water and receive the health and wholeness Jesus brings, we can drop our water pots and move on with our life. That is good news—the Gospel! You don't have to stay stuck in the painful past of empty, lifeless, broken relationships. Jesus will heal every place you have been hurt and satisfy the thirst of your soul, which man cannot do.

Recognize Toxic Relationships and Know When to Walk Away

When God wants to bless you, He sends a person into your life. When Satan wants to mess you up, he sends a person into your life. God does not come down in a glory cloud or in the form of a dove and sit on top of your head while you're eating your breakfast cereal. God comes to you through people. He uses people. And the devil doesn't come to you with a pitchfork and two horns and a tail, looking like Jason Voorhees or Freddy Krueger and saying, "I'm going to get you today." He comes through people. Relationships are the currency of the kingdom.

God desires to give you a spirit of wisdom and discernment so you can discern which people in your life are assets and those who are liabilities who is safe and who is unsafe. If you were to look at your life in terms of your "net worth"—not in financial terms, but your value as a person—you might be surprised to discover that your net worth is determined in large measure by your network. We are largely products of the people whom we are around. If you show me your friends, I'll show you your value system.

"Do not be so deceived and misled! Evil companionships (communion, associations) corrupt and deprave good manners and morals and character" (1 Corinthians 15:33 AMP). The failure in a person's life to accomplish and achieve the big things they desire or to cultivate the greatness within them is often a result of the failure to understand the power of "next"—the value of building relationships connected to your life on the basis of love, respect, acceptance, loyalty, honor, and trust. We are all influenced by the impact that people "next" to us have had on our lives. To be next to someone means to "be adjacent, near, or close." When you are close, you have contact, which is where the connection is made and through which impartation occurs. Show me who is close or next to you, and I will show you what is going into you. As is true of electricity, a contact is the passage through which electricity flows. Impartation determines output. What comes out of me is a result of what is going into me. This is why Proverbs 13:20 declares: "He who walks with wise men will be wise, but the companion of fools will be destroyed."

With the understanding of this principle, it is vital to examine in an objective manner the quality and character of the relationships in your life. No relationship will be perfect or flawless. In fact, it is the differences and imperfections that can create opportunity for personal growth and maturity. However, there are relationships that are toxic for you and end up being detrimental and damaging to your well-being. These are liabilities.

There are several types of relationships you need to identify as liabilities. I want to focus on three relationships you need to consider.

Liability #1
Relationships That Create Constant Disagreement and Strife

In Amos 3:3, the prophet says, "Can two walk together, unless they are agreed?" Such a wise observation loaded with profound implications for relationships. If you and I are trying to get to the same destination, and we need to walk together, how can I walk with you unless we have the power of agreement going? Now, agreement is so powerful that God says if two of you agree in prayer as touching anything in heaven and earth, it will be done (Matthew 18:18–20). Agreement is so powerful that God says a house divided cannot stand—if there is division, there is a collapse of the foundation (Mark 3:25).

Agreed is one of the most underestimated and overlooked words in all of the Scripture. In Amos 3:3, *agreed* means to "fix upon by agreement or appointment, to meet at a stated time, and to direct in a certain quarter or position." With agreement, we are united. Without it, we are divided. By the power of agreement, truth is established, and when truth is established, covenant can be formed. There can be no covenant or bonding or real relationship without truth.

So, if I am going to succeed, I need to be dealing with people who come to terms through negotiation, and we agree. That way we can stay on the same pathway. If my business, my family, my ministry, or my network of friends is going to succeed, there has to be the power of agreement. That does not mean the absence of some good, healthy conflict at times. We can have healthy disagreements as long as we are able to work our way through them and find resolution. But God is a God of order, and He does not bless out of His order. We are to labor to keep the bond of unity in our relationships. (Eph 4:1-6)

We also have to realize there is dangerous, unhealthy conflict. "For where envy and self-seeking exist, confusion and every evil thing are there" (James 3:16). Where there is a faction or a pulling away or strife, there is confusion. "Confusion" means instability and a state of disorder, and watch what else James mentions—"and every evil thing."

If the enemy can get your life into disorder, then

there is instability, which has serious consequences. James 1:7–8 says, "For let not that man suppose that he will receive anything from the Lord; he is a double-minded man, unstable in all his ways." When I get out of order and there's instability, I have given the enemy legal entryway into my life by breaking the pattern and principles of God. Many people who are frustrated by not seeing the promises of God come to pass in their life often don't understand that provision can only occur by being in proper position, which is the divine accurate order and arrangement of things.

> "People are lonely because they build walls instead of bridges."
> —JOSEPH F. NEWTON

God is a God of order and structure and government. "And the government will be upon His shoulder. And His name will be called Wonderful, Counselor, Mighty God, Everlasting Father, Prince of Peace" (Isaiah 9:6). Read through Psalm 133: "Behold, how good and how pleasant it is for brethren to dwell together in unity! It is like the precious oil upon the head, running down on the beard, the beard of Aaron, running down on the edge of his garments. It is like the dew of Hermon, descending upon the mountains of Zion; for there the LORD commanded the blessing—life forevermore." "In unity," God says, He has a commanded blessing. So often we don't see the blessing of God in our life because of the self-serving agenda's, rebellion and division. Perhaps that is why Jesus prayed in His final moments on earth that His disciples might "be made perfect in one" (John 17:23).

This is precisely why the apostle Paul admonished the Ephesian church: "Endeavoring to keep the unity of the Spirit in the bond of peace" (Ephesians 4:3).

We are all presented with opportunities that can create division or bring unity. When you hear accusations or rumors or see a vulnerable time in another person's life, you can choose to pour fuel and flame the fire or pour water and stop the fire. You can choose to be a reconciler and peacemaker or an agitator and menace.

Either way, I have this to remember: whatever I sow in life is what I reap in life (Galatians 6:7). If I lack wholeness and make the move to take advantage of a person's situation, the day will come when I reap the same or similar. If I am healthy and in the order God has ordained, I will choose to be a peacemaker and bless their life, and on a day when I need it, I will reap the same. A word to the wise: instant gratification is not worth the long-term harvest you are going to yield by being divisive in your life.

Liability #2
Relationships That Hide You, Hold You to Your Past, and Hinder Your Growth

The second type of toxic relationship is the type that

says, "I knew you when . . ." If you read the fascinating account recorded in Matthew 13:54–58, it says Jesus could not do many miracles in His hometown because they thought of Him merely as Joseph's boy. Jesus, the Son of God, was limited here because they said, "He's just the carpenter's son. We know His mother and brothers and sisters." These people are limited because they keep holding on to something God has told them to release. They nurture something from the past that needs to be cut off.

I'm not talking, of course, of relationships that you have entered into with a covenant or relationships God has ordained for your life. You can't just casually walk away from a father or mother or spouse or child. I'm talking about friendships and business associations and casual acquaintances and distant relatives who remind you continually of what people used to think of you. These old opinions were never God's opinions and are opinions that do not relate to your tomorrow. They relate only to your yesterday.

When a space shuttle takes off, the rocket boosters that provide the initial lift to propel the shuttle through the earth's atmosphere fall off at a certain point or they will destroy the shuttle. Some of us hold on to relationships and things that were meant as boosters in our life, when God has said they were meant only for a season. What was a lifter becomes a weight in your life. There are some people in your past whom God says you've got to walk away from, because they're holding you to a certain mentality that will never allow you to get where God wants you to go. They keep pulling you back down.

Philippians 3:13–14 says, "Forgetting those things which are behind and reaching forward to those things which are ahead, I press toward the goal for the prize of the upward call of God in Christ Jesus." Proverbs 4:25 says, "Let your eyes look straight ahead, and your eyelids look right before you." You cannot keep looking backward and forward at the same time. Some of you need to break the rearview mirror. You need to get rid of some of those songs you keep playing and that old scrapbook, because they pull you right back into your old lifestyle.

It's time to move on from ancient history. You can waste years of your life by being stuck in the past, and you eliminate what God has for your future by holding on to what you had in your past. Let go and let God move you ahead.

Some people are afraid to let go of the past because it takes them out of the familiar. But just because something is not familiar doesn't mean it's not good for you. Until the Israelites crossed the Jordan, they did not know what the grapes of Canaan tasted like. The onions and the leeks of Egypt were good, but when they tasted the produce of Canaan, they wondered what they ever liked about Egypt.

A common past is good. It unites our yesterdays. But

common goals are better because they unite our tomorrows. It's not about where have we been, but where are we going? And if you can't connect with people who are going where you're going, then you're going to ultimately have problems.

Liability #3
Relationships That Are Violators of the Heart and Head

Probably the most dangerous relationships are predators of the heart. The Bible says, "Keep your heart with all diligence, for out of it spring the issues of life" (Proverbs 4:23). Here is a delicate challenge. If I put up too high of a wall around my heart, I become a prisoner to myself. It is easy for me to isolate myself from the good relationships God has for me, because I've been wounded in the past. But if I'm not guarded at all, I'm vulnerable to the wounding of the enemy. And so I have to be responsible to guard my heart.

For instance, the Bible tells us to "not believe every spirit, but test the spirits" in other people before we ever get into a relationship with them (1 John 4:1). This means we shouldn't jump into a relationship quickly, whether it's with a person or an organization. It takes time to really know another person or a group of people. You shouldn't make a decision based on one experience, because you're only seeing a sliver of the person or group. Anybody can show you a side they want you to see for a time. How many people wake up one day and wonder who the person lying next to them is? Often people have "purchased" something based on false or misleading advertising. They didn't pay attention to the fine print. Saturate a potential relationship in prayer and ask God to reveal to you if they are sent by Him. Remember that character is more important than gifting. Do they display and seek to walk in the fruit of the Spirit? (Gal 5:22)

I have a responsibility to guard my heart, but not to imprison it. Predators of the heart are so dangerous because they prey on your heart and rob you of control. Predators are usually the nicest, most charismatic, outgoing people, but they say what you want to hear, not what you need to hear. They see your vulnerabilities, your weaknesses, and your needs. They turn on the charm, hand out their checkbook, and will go to great lengths in order to win you and to control you.

Taking advantage of your need to be loved and accepted, predators manipulate you to get what they want and need from you. Listen up: never lose your identity or compromise your character for anyone! If they don't like you, all of you, just the way you are, then walk away. You cannot lose who you are for them. You will wreck yourself trying to be someone or something you're not. And ultimately, if they will sin with you, they'll sin against you. What they do now, they'll do later without a true conversion and transformation. Don't deceive yourself into thinking that person will never do it to you.

"So," you ask, "why do I keep attracting violators and being attracted to them?" Because if you are masochistic as I have been, where you tend to allow yourself to be used and abused by not saying no or having healthy boundaries, and setting yourself up to get hurt, victimized, or taken advantage of, you've probably taken on a mentality that says "I must have done something to deserve this." You have developed a self-defeating behavior pattern that you consciously or unconsciously indulge in. It goes back to the erroneous messaging directing and dictating our beliefs about ourselves and others.

When you've been wounded or abused in life, you believe subconsciously that you deserve the kind of treatment predators deal out. You are very vulnerable to people who prey on your needs and your weaknesses, because you are leaking out life. Whatever gets deposited in you doesn't stay in you. Until you've experienced the intimacy of God, and He brings healing and wholeness to every place you've been wounded and hurt, you won't recognize all the lies you've believed or how to defeat the predators. Once you are strengthened within yourself and you can function fully, because you understand who you are and you've overcome your condition by knowing your position in Christ Jesus, you won't devalue yourself for anybody who is out to take advantage of you.

Relationships are vital to our wholeness and to our full functionality. And yet they can be very complicated, very complex, especially with self-centered, self-interested violators that take advantage of people for their own interests. Knowledge is power when you put knowledge to use. "In all your getting, get understanding" (Proverbs 4:7). Learn how to recover from the abuse of your past and how to recognize the tendencies and traits that lead to harmful behavior from unsafe people.

Your life conditions may be bad, and you may have grown up with a mentality that is "bad, bad, bad." But if you don't deal with it, it will continue to eliminate all the good that God has for you. It's when you stop living in rebellion and disobedience to the Word of God that you begin to see the result of God in your life. And God has such good things for you. Yes, He has good relationships for you. He has a good life for you. He has blessings for you. He says, "With long life I will satisfy him, and show him My salvation" (Psalm 91:16). Every day God wants you satisfied.

So toss out the lie that you have to live the rest of your life with bad days and broken relationships. The God of our salvation says, "Blessed be the Lord, Who daily loads us with benefits" (Psalm 68:19). God is constantly thinking about how He can bless you, and He has every good and perfect gift for you (James 1:17). I'm not talking about a "sugar-daddy" mentality that demands provision for service. I'm talking about real bona fide blessing in your life where God says, "I have good things for you as you mature in your ability to handle them." God is a loving, gentle, good provider for all the needs in your life.

Cast out any lies that contradict the nature and character of God as revealed in His Word and embrace the truth. God is working in your life to bring you nothing but good. If you haven't found your spouse yet, be patient. It's not that God doesn't have a spouse for you; it's that He's doing a work in that person's life and in yours. And you don't want that man or woman right now, trust me, if God is still purging and purifying him or her. Perhaps you are not ready for the responsibility that relationship will bring with it. Be patient and let God do what God needs to do, so God can complete what God wants to complete.

"Trust in the Lord with all your heart, and lean not on your own understanding; in all your ways acknowledge Him, and He shall direct your paths" (Proverbs 3:5–6).

God is doing a work in your life so you can be positioned for what He has purposed for you. And He wants to develop healthy relationships by developing healthiness in you. We were created for intimacy, to connect with someone with heart, soul and mind. Intimacy occurs when we are open, vulnerable, and honest, for these qualities help us to connect in closeness.

Healthy Relationships in the Body of Christ

If there is one place where you would hope to experience healthy relationships, it is within the body of Christ, which is the family of God. It is clear that when God wants to bless you, He sends a person into your life. For your dream and your destiny to be fulfilled, you need the association and stimulation of a significant person or significant people who have the ability to stir up the dream and destiny on the inside of you.

When we commit ourselves to functioning in the church, we must deal with the issue of people and find ways to connect in order to build the kingdom of God. We are many members of one Body. The reality is that it's not always smooth sailing in our relationships within the church. In fact, you may have someone you know at church who has deeply wounded or offended you. Within any group of people, you will always have personality differences, communication barriers, and difficulties to overcome.

While it is much easier to come into an intimate place and position of relationship with the Lord, which is really not your challenge, we must learn to love and live with one another as God desires. God is good and merciful. God is so good and merciful that He covers for you and protects you when He could expose and hurt you. When God wrestles with you, He does it privately, as He did with Jacob (Genesis 32:22–32). God is so awesome. He doesn't embarrass you or shame you. Every single day God is mindful of you, thinking about you. If you make your bed in hell, He'll find you there (Psalm 139:8). Getting along with God is not the challenge.

Our problem is getting along with people. So how do you get along with people, especially God's people? How should you?

Consider these words from the apostle Paul as he speaks about the church and our relationships:

> **"Security in a relationship lies neither in looking back to what it was, nor forward to what it might be, but living in the present and accepting it as it is now."**
> —ANNE LINDBERGH

Therefore you are no longer outsiders (exiles, migrants, and aliens, excluded from the rights of citizens), but you now share citizenship with the saints (God's own people, consecrated and set apart for Himself); and you belong to God's [own] household. You are built upon the foundation of the apostles and prophets with Christ Jesus Himself the chief Cornerstone. In Him the whole structure is joined (bound, welded) together harmoniously, and it continues to rise (grow, increase) into a holy temple in the Lord [a sanctuary dedicated, consecrated, and sacred to the presence of the Lord]. In Him [and in fellowship with one another] you yourselves also are being built up [into this structure] with the rest, to form a fixed abode (dwelling place) of God in (by, through) the Spirit.

Ephesians 2:19–22 amp

Note that Paul said, "In Him [and in fellowship with one another] you yourselves also are being built up [into this structure]." In the fellowship of the church, we are living stones being built into a wall, and Jesus is the Chief Cornerstone. Now, a stone is very different from a smooth cement block. A stone is jagged and rough and dirty and not necessarily symmetrical. It's easy to look at stones . . . and other believers . . . and say they can't be a part of the wall because they're just not right or perfect enough. After all, how do the stones jointly fit together with their irregularities and jagged points? The secret is that God has to do a smoothing away to make them fit. The wall does not change for the stone; the stone must change for the wall.

"In Him the whole structure is joined (bound, welded) together harmoniously." And so God is buffeting some things out of your life. He is taking you through a process. He is causing you to be in a situation where you will find out what's really in you. He is allowing you under pressure to discover whether you really have the love of God inside of you. Is it really unconditional love? Is it compassion? (Compassion is loving someone with the foreknowledge that they will potentially hurt and harm you.) Is the love of God operating in you, or is there envy and jealousy? Is there arrogance and self-righteousness? Is there pride, resentfulness, or bitterness?

Watch what the apostle Paul says: note that "you" are being built up by the fellowship of one another, not simply by the people whom you like and get along with but by all people. In other words, God is using that person who is plucking your last nerve as well as the person empowering you to build you into your place in the body of Christ. Choose to love and minister to those whom God has brought into your life. Instead of running from them, tell them God has good things for them. Love them, bless them, and always pray for them.

And so He says, "I want you to begin to build healthy relationships, because I am building a wall so I can see My body do what they are called to do." You are a part of a bigger picture with a responsibility to love one another.

So how do I begin to sort through the relationships in my life, relinquishing the unhealthy ones and building up the ones that God has called to me? How do I build healthy relationships?

CHAPTER EIGHT

Nine Keys *to* Healthy Relationships

Key #1
to Healthy Relationships

Identify and Accept the Reality of Your Relationships

How would describe the health of your relationships? Be honest, because it's crucial for your life. Friend, you cannot conquer what you don't confront, and you cannot confront what you don't identify. Many people live in denial or repression. They continually say, "Everything is okay. It's okay. We get along wonderful." But it's not okay.

Each person has been engaged in hiding many thoughts and feelings from himself, often for a long period of time. *Denial* is an unconscious act. It can be defined as "a way of resolving emotional conflict and its anxiety by the unconscious detachment of thoughts that would be otherwise unbearable."

It order to bring resolution or restoration to any relationship, we must deal with it through honest, unbiased assessment. To relinquish the unhealthy, you have to admit to yourself when something is not functioning. If you are presently involved in relationships that prey on your heart and rob you of control over your life, it's time to make a change. Trust God to help you recognize when a relationship is becoming detrimental to you, to your purpose, or to the health and well-being of those you love.

There are four types of relationships in your life—those that add, those that subtract, those that multiply, and those that divide. And so when something becomes divisive, or when something is subtracting, you have to look at the reality of that relationship and say, "It's not working," which means one of three things.

Number one, that relationship was only for a season. Like those rocket boosters that lift you into the first atmosphere, they must fall off if you're going to make it to the next level. You keep trying to hold on to the relationship, but God is saying, "It's time for that relationship to fall off. I'm trying to get you to the next stratosphere, but if you try to hang on to those boosters, they will actually pull you back down and destroy you." Some relationships are there for a season, but if you hold on past their longevity, what was once delightful will become destructive. In wanting to offer ourselves stability and grounding, many of us lose our balance and objectivity. We become confused and have those blurred boundaries when discerning what to let go of and what to hold on to, when to let go and when to hold on. King Solomon, with great wisdom, confirmed that there is a time for everything. (Ecc. 3:5,6) "a time to scatter stones and a time to gather them, a time to embrace and a time to refrain from embracing, a time to search, and a time to give up, a time to keep and a time to throw away".

Number two, that relationship is one that God says you have to leave because the person will hold you to an old mentality and lifestyle. We saw this clearly in the call of Abraham. God told him to leave his country, his family, and his father's house and go to a land that He would show him (Genesis 12:1). Some people will hold you to your past, so you have to leave. They will subtract and divide your life. You have to be real with yourself and the relationship and ask, "What do I do to move ahead to the place that God has for me?"

> "A relationship isn't meant to be an insurance policy, a life preserver, or a security blanket."
> —DIANE CROWLEY

If you continue to hold on to a relationship that is no longer a part of God's plan, then you will never fulfill the purpose that God has for you. You are trying to rehabilitate something that God is finished with. You cannot revive something that God says is not going to work. Do not be afraid to let go and surrender a relationship for fear of being alone. God will never leave or forsake you.

Number three, if you think you're going to be able to change that person and take them with you, you are deceiving yourself. You are lying to yourself. People change, but not much. The Bible says, "Can the Ethiopian change his skin or the leopard its spots? Then may you also do good who are accustomed to do evil" (Jeremiah 13:23). The only way someone can change is through the Word of God that sanctifies and washes them, and you cannot force-feed the Word if they're not hungry. All you can do is pray that God will get them in a place where they are starving for the Word, because the Word will transform them.

If you want to change your way of living, you've got to change your way of thinking. But until you are sick and tired of being sick and tired, you're not going to change your way of thinking. And so, you can never change somebody else. You have to accept that person for who they are and recognize who they are. Acceptance is the starting point of any healthy relationship.

I have met singles who think that if they just get married, they can change their partner. To that I say, "The devil is a liar." In fact, marriage will probably only magnify what is already there.

Here's a principle we need to grasp: unconditional love and compassion is accepting a person for exactly who they are and recognizing that God is doing the work in their life. We have to be ready to pay the price for allowing God to work in their life in His way. Perhaps you feel God has used you in the past to help change someone, but you sense it was for a season. Releasing someone does not mean they will not get better. It means God is better suited for the job than you are. And bringing closure does not mean it's final. It means you are giving them over to God.

Key #2
to Healthy Relationships
Don't Try to Be Someone Else's God

There's a huge difference between helping a person and carrying a person. You aren't the Holy Spirit. Don't enter into an enabling relationship in which you come to feel totally responsible for a person's success or failure.

It is easy to move from caring into "carrying." The weight we often bear is not our responsibility. You must remind yourself that you are not to take on the "God complex" by trying to fix what you are not supposed to. There are times that we are to give people over to God for them to feel and face the consequences of their decisions. Examine closely the relationships in your life, especially if you are always trying to help or rescue others who are in trouble. As long as we're trying to make sure they are okay all the time, we're trying to be their God. Because of our need to be needed, we get in the way of God doing what He wants to do. And so you have to get out of the way for God to do the work He wants to do.

In fact, the truest form of the word submission means to "duck" (my paraphrase). Are you standing in the way of God doing a work in someone's life because you have taken on responsibilities and needs that don't belong to you?

Some of us keep getting in the way of God doing what He wants to do in our spouse or our child or our boss or our best friend. God may tell you that every time you give it over to Him, then you pick it back up and try to fix it yourself. So, duck. Get out of the way. First Peter 5:7 says, "Casting all your care upon Him, for He cares for you." To "cast" means to roll it over and give it to God and then leave it there. Give it over and don't pick it up again, but leave it in the hands of God. And know that God is more qualified and better at doing the job and getting it done than you are. God knows exactly how to visit a person and how to change and transform them. Jesus never yelled, shamed or withdrew from anyone to discipline them. He taught with love, limits and consequences.

And in all your relationships, don't demand from people what only God can give. Only God can give you a deep awareness of how infinitely valuable and precious you are to Him, and what a glorious destiny He has for you. Only God can see and meet the unfulfilled needs in your life that even you don't recognize. Only God can fix your heart. Only God can mend your mind. Recognize that no other human being can ever complete you, and you'll save yourself a world of disappointment.

Key #3
to Healthy Relationships
Don't Fear Criticism

So what happens when we start to deal with these unhealthy relationships that don't bring us into the purpose God has for us? When you begin to grow and mature and get away from the unhealthy relationships, you better become comfortable with criticism. Why? Because not everybody is going to be happy about your decision. You cannot please all people all the time. People are going to take a hit at you in order to defend, justify, or protect themselves.

To break away from unhealthy relationships, you need to be comfortable in your own skin and confident enough to know who you are and the God whom you serve. There are people who are going to try to pull you back. The loss of whatever you've been giving some people is going to make them upset. Others simply hate your success, achievement, and growth. It rubs salt in the wound of their failure.

When you begin to walk away from unhealthy relationships, people who have controlled you, manipulated you, used you, abused you, and know how to pull all the strings that keep you in that unhealthy relationship are going to increase the pressure. They won't give up without a fight. And when they see you becoming whole and healthy, it becomes a mirror reflection of their sickness and their dysfunction, which will make them angry.

You will need to be rock solid in your conviction that you deserve better because God has shown you better. When you know better in your heart, you do better. And so you can say, "I love you, but I can't live with you this way. I love you, but I can't compromise my character for anybody. I like you, but I'm not going to forfeit my destiny. So I'm going to let God deal with you as God is dealing with me, and you can call me whatever you want. Do whatever you want to do. Say whatever you want to say. I really don't care. I'm going to love you. I'm not going to retaliate, because I am trusting God to take care of me as well as you."

Here's a visual of what you'll face. If you've ever seen

a pot of live crabs, you know that when one crab starts trying to climb out of the pot, the other crabs try to latch hold of it and pull it back down. As you are getting healthy and pulling yourself out of the pot, most of the people in your life are not going to say, "Here's my hand, help me out, too." No, most of them are going to grab you by your foot and try to yank you back down. You have to have the utter conviction that you are going where God tells you to go. You're going to do what God says you can do. You're going to have what God says you can have.

Trust God to give you the courage to end the relationship, and then trust Him to give you broad shoulders and thick enough skin to take the criticism you may face for ending the relationship.

Key #4
to Healthy Relationships
Develop a Budget for Each Level of Your Relationships

The fourth thing you have to do is develop a budget for each level of your relationships. Every relationship works better for both people when there are dimensions of the relationship that are established from the beginning. In other words, you have to know what the expectations and roles of responsibility are. How much are you pouring in or depositing into this relationship, and what do you expect and desire to receive from them?

Determine how far you are willing to go and how much you are willing to invest in that relationship. It is wise to get to know somebody very well before you enter into a covenant or long-term relationship, whether that's a marriage, a business, or a friendship. Take your time before making any permanent decisions.

Sometimes, we only are exposed to one dimension of a person. They are multifaceted. Anybody can falsely market themselves for a season, and, unfortunately, people do it all the time. They sell themselves as beautiful, quiet, meek, and laid back. Then two years into the marriage they have an "in your face" attitude.

The Bible uses the word "wait" more than 150 times, often referring to one's relationship with God. Therefore, how much more do we need to wait and fully go through the different stages of healthy bonding to have good attachments in our relationships. Remember that God is never in a hurry. It is line upon line, precept upon precept. The enemy, however, is hasty, fast, and corrupt. "I have to do it right now! I'm in love! I'm in love! I'm in love!" I'm sorry to burst that bubble, but maybe that is just lust. Let it pass. You'll be okay. You will even be grateful that you did not embrace a permanent decision in a temporary season of your life.

When you are entering into a covenant relationship, you need to develop a budget. That means you take into consideration the assets and the deficits, the withdrawals and the deposits. You must know the limits for what you can give, what you will be able to withdraw, and see if it "balances" out.

In relationships where you do all the giving, if you don't have a place or a person or something that is restoring you and replenishing you, you will pay a huge price. You might not physically die, but there are areas in your life that are dying right now because you are always giving out and never receiving back.

> **"Whenever you're in conflict with someone, there is one factor that can make the difference between damaging your relationship and deepening it. That factor is attitude"**
> —WILLIAM JAMES

Granted, there are times when there are people in life to whom you are assigned to give, give, and give. But every once in a while, whether it is for an hour, a day, or a month, you need to be separated from them. There is a time for giving to and caring for and nurturing, and there is a time you need to be revived, replenished, and nourished yourself.

When you provide care for another person, you experience different pressures. Sometimes they are external, and other times they originate from within. For instance, you may have additional stress unrelated to the individual you are caring for that puts you at the risk for overload. Maybe you impose pressure on yourself by expecting that regardless of the number of kinds of responsibilities you must fulfill, you should be able to carry them forth without letting anyone down. There must be places for you to refuel and recharge in order for you to be effective in your giving to others.

Maintaining God ordained relationships that replenish and balance you is vital to avoid burnout.

You also need to realize that the more you are responsible for in life, the smaller your circle gets. The more you grow in God, the smaller your circle gets. For example, when God gave the Law to the children of Israel, over three million people were all around at the base of the mountain. When Moses and Joshua started going up the mountain, Joshua only went halfway up. The higher Moses went, the smaller the circle became, until ultimately he was the only one at the top (Exodus 19). When you grow and go up higher in life, you have more responsibility in life, and your circle will get smaller.

As you mature spiritually and take on more responsibility, you will need to learn how to sustain yourself and pour life back into yourself. You need to learn to speak "to one another in psalms and hymns and spiritual songs, singing and making melody in your heart to the Lord" (Ephesians 5:19). You will transition off the dependency of other people and discover how to sustain your life more independently. I am not saying you don't need other people, because you do. However, when God is calling you to a higher level, you will find yourself in a position where you must know how to "feed yourself."

Key #5
to Healthy Relationships
Progressively End Unhealthy Relationships

So what do you do with these unhealthy relationships? You end them progressively. *Progressively.* In other words, don't ever burn a bridge unless it's mandatory. When you dissolve a relationship, don't do so in anger or bitterness.

There is a right way and a wrong way to end a relationship. Paul and Barnabas show us the right way in Acts 15:36–41. In the midst of a mission trip, Paul and Barnabas reached an impasse over whether Mark should come with them. The two men had ministered together for a long while, but "the contention became so sharp that they parted from one another" (v. 39). I'm sure the first thing they did was seek God through prayer. Whenever you're going to end a relationship, you need to do it through prayer. And although they wanted the best for each other, the conclusion was that the best decision was to separate and both groups would continue to preach the Gospel.

Was that the right way to end the relationship? We do know that later in the Book of Acts they came back together and worked together. Had they not ended the relationship correctly, there would have been such a wounding that they could not have come back together and accomplished what they did for the Kingdom of God. When there is too much damage and wounding, you will be so guarded that you will never be able to come back in that relationship and maybe not into any relationship that even feels similar to it. So there is a right way to exit and there is a wrong way.

When you exit a relationship, you should do so with mutual respect and love. Ideally, you want to be able to say, "Even though we're parting ways, I want the best for you, and you want the best for me, and I'm going to bless you in Jesus' name. I want to do you good, and I am going to do you right, and I'm going to leave all the rest in the hands of God."

You don't walk out casually on committed relationships that God has brought together. After much counsel and attempts that have failed and exhaustion of all possibilities, there are relationships that by the Word of God you can walk away from and recognize that season is over. Don't try to force what no longer fits. It's time for you to move to a different place. When there is potential harm or danger, you should never subject yourself to it, but get out of the situation and immediately seek help.

Here's the other thing about progressively ending relationships. Don't end all your unhealthy relationships at once, because it is too stressful. It takes emotional energy to end a relationship, and if you cut every unhealthy relationship out of your life at one time, you are likely to be overwhelmed by the loss. Cut unhealthy relationships out of your life one at a time until you can look around and say, "All of my relationships are pleasing to God."

Key #6
to Healthy Relationships
Don't Revisit a Relationship You Have Decided to End

One big relationship problem for some people is they keep going back to what God has finished. Don't revisit what God has decided to end. When it is over, it is over. The biblical principle is: "No one, having put his hand to the plow, and looking back, is fit for the kingdom of God" (Luke 9:62). Don't revisit what God has finished. It's over. It brings us back to James 1:7–8: "For let not that man suppose that he will receive anything from the Lord; he is a double-minded man, unstable in all his ways." If we keep trying to hold on to what God is through with and simultaneously grab what God is opening to us, we are unstable and go nowhere. You cannot continue to revisit your past and try to drag it into your future. Philippians 3:13 says, "Forgetting those

> **"If we are incapable of finding peace in ourselves, it is pointless to search elsewhere."**
> —FRANCOIS DE LA ROCHEFOUCAULD

things which are behind and reaching forward to those things which are ahead." So you have to let go of the old so you can embrace the new.

If you try to hold on to past relationships, you end up living a suspended life. Job 7:6 describes it clearly: "My days . . . are spent without hope." To be in a place of suspension is the most frustrating place to live. God is a progressive God, and He calls you to live from glory to glory (2 Corinthians 3:18). When you are suspended, you are frustrated because you feel like you're being pulled back and forth and never going anywhere.

When God says it's over, don't revisit it. "As a dog returns to his own vomit, so a fool repeats his folly" (Proverbs 26:11). Ooh! That's heavy! Don't be foolish. When God says it's over, let it go and trust that God has more for you and your future than there ever was in your past. Trust that God is good, and just because you haven't seen it yet doesn't mean it's not going to be good.

Don't be afraid because the new relationships that God moves you into feel unfamiliar. Ask the Lord to give you His *shalom* or *peace*, where nothing is missing, nothing is broken in your future. " 'The glory of this latter temple shall be greater than the former,' says the Lord of hosts. 'And in this place I will give peace,' says the Lord of hosts" (Haggai 2:9). Great shall be your peace. You have to trust that what God has ahead of you is so much greater than anything behind you.

At this point, it would be worth your while to read the biblical story of Ruth. She was born into a bad situation, with a dysfunctional past, and grew up in the heathen land of Moab during the period when the judges ruled Israel. She was exposed to a highly perverse culture and the worst forms of human behavior.

Ruth became the wife of Chilion, the son of Elimelech and Naomi. Elimelech was a Jewish farmer from Bethlehem who had come to Moab with his wife and two sons to escape a severe famine in Judah. Both of their sons—Mahlon and Chilion—married Moabite girls. The older son married a woman named Orpah. The younger son married Ruth. Mahlon and Chilion were apparently prone to sickness. Mahlon's name means "puny," and Chilion's name means "unhealthy."

Both of these men died young, and Elimelech also died. Naomi found herself a widow with two widowed daughters-in-law. Facing her bitter options, Naomi decides to return to Bethlehem and presses her daughters-in-law to remain in Moab and find new husbands. Basically, Naomi tells the two young Moabite women, "You don't know what's ahead of you, but you know what's behind you, so stay back. Go back to your mothers, and may God bless you for your kindness to me."

But Ruth says, " 'Entreat me not to leave you, or to turn back from following after you; for wherever you go, I will go; and wherever you lodge, I will lodge; your people shall be my people, and your God, my God. Where you die, I will die, and there will I be buried' " (Ruth 1:16-17). In other words, Ruth says, "I'm going to go where I've never been to get what I've never had."

And she follows Ruth back to Bethlehem, because Bethlehem is the place of blessing where God has her future husband, Boaz. However, Boaz is not just her husband-to-be; he is the blessing from God. And if you follow the love story, you discover that Ruth does not have to put bait on her hook to get Boaz. She doesn't have to compromise herself. All she has to do is obey God and follow the instruction of God, and God brings Boaz. Boaz notices her because God's favor is on her. God will always have the people who are assigned to be a blessing in your life to notice you.

> "Now I think everyone should ask, 'Am I going to be able to be the person I want to be in this relationship?'"
> —ALI MACGRAW

This shows why you don't have to manipulate your way into someone's life. You don't have to be a people pleaser. You don't have to sleep your way to the top. You don't have to conive your way in. God will always have people who are to be a blessing in your life notice you. All you have to do is be productive in what God has called you to do, and you will be noticed.

Boaz meets Ruth in Bethlehem, and the blessing of God is there. Why? Because Ruth did not revisit her past.

She made no provision to go back to her old relationships. She didn't buy a camel train ticket back to Moab in case Boaz wasn't in Bethlehem. She didn't have a plan C, D, and E in case A and B didn't work out. God says, "Let go of the relationships I'm finished with because part of your destiny also includes bringing closure to your past."

Ruth is proof that it doesn't matter where you start in life; it matters where you finish. In the light of her past and the events of her present, there was something great about Ruth—she rose above her past. She could have easily looked at Naomi's bitter experience and decided to stay back in Moab and hide in her past. But Ruth determined she was going to get out of her past and into her future with the God of Israel.

It wasn't Naomi's shining personality that she followed; it was the principle of God's blessing. Some of us follow people because of their personality, not because of principle. That's why we better have an ear to hear what the Spirit of God is saying. God deals more with principle than He does with personality.

> God has a life coach for you.
> God has a mentor for you.
> God has a pastor for you.
> God has good friends for you.
> God has a family for you.
> God has great relationships for you.
> God has a spouse for you.

But if you keep holding on to relationships that were meant to be in the past, it's as though you keep drinking from a defiled, wasted, contaminated, nuclear stream. Break the water pot! Don't wean yourself off. Make no provision for the past. Don't add something to which you can keep going back. Shut that door. Rip up the little black book. Throw away the phone number. The day you make a decision, it's over.

By holding on to the past, you eliminate what God has for you. I wish I could take you right into the blessings of all the healthy relationships that God has for you. You have to understand that in order to get there, you have to not only recognize, identify, and accept the reality of the unhealthy relationships, but also do something about the unhealthy relationships.

Why don't you commit this to God right now? Pray this prayer with me: "God, bring the right people into my life . . . and remove the wrong people. Help me accept the reality of all of my relationships by doing a budget or an audit of the wells from which I'm drinking. Today, I make a decision, with the help of the Holy Spirit, to break and drop every water pot that would have me drinking out of the wrong well. In the name of Jesus, I decree this, I declare this, and it is established."

And I am praying that the right people, the right associations, are coming into your life. The right people are going to find you and favor you. It doesn't matter where you are or what the situation is, because the Lord is not limited. There is going to be something that causes you to be magnified and stand out. God is going to favor you with the right people.

There is a destiny, there is a plan, there is a purpose over your life, and you need the association of the right people for the stimulation of the dream or vision that is inside of you. May God bring them to you in the name of Jesus. Even the people who are to buffet you and cut off the rough edges of your character are good. You'll know because you will have the peace of God, the fruit of the Spirit working in your life.

Key #7
to Healthy Relationships
Form Relationships That Fit

In order to develop healthy relationships that create and achieve success, we have to recognize what right partnerships look like. When something "fits," it is "well-suited," as a tailor-made suit is formed for you. Every dream you have needs the right people in order for it to be birthed into reality. No one succeeds alone. You must have the right team operating in their unique giftings that know how to work together toward a common vision or destiny.

There is a fundamental fact about the makeup of the human personality: most people function best when teamed up with at least one other person. If you find one other person to join you in your endeavors, you can double your capabilities, which creates exponential increase.

Relationships are most productive when we interact with people who complement us without duplicating us. In other words, you need to cross-pollinate. You need to get with people who are not exactly like you but still complement you. By that, I mean they are similar in values, beliefs, etc., yet diverse in strengths, giftings, knowledge, and exposure. Continual conflict will ultimately cause division. For results, there must be cooperation and congruency. Efforts are best achieved where there is collaboration. While you maintain a joint effort, your diversities continue to educate and expose each other to new skills, perspectives, and practices.

You need to be exposed to different things in life in order to be equipped for the assignment of God on your life. You need to get into conversations that intimidate you. You need to go into brand-new situations about which you have no understanding and learn from them. You cannot be so intimidated and insecure that you miss out on the valuable lessons they can teach you.

Think about this. If the young shepherd David had been insecure, he could not have received the training he received from the king's son Jonathan that equipped him for the palace that he was destined to rule. David was anointed to be a prophet, priest, and king, and Jonathan was trained in everything that David was not. Jonathan recognized the anointing of God was on David and was humble enough to take off his cloak of royalty and say, "God has chosen you for the position, but as much as I need you because you are chosen by God, you need me because I've been trained by man." Together they cultivated and greatly advanced the plan of God.

Or consider the life of Moses. He was a Jewish boy who had to be trained in Pharaoh's daughter's palace in order to function in the position God had for him.

You need to get out of your life box and sphere. You need to get out of your little world and find out there is a huge world out there that is so distinctly different. You see, your covenant relationships cannot all be exactly like you.

> "Do not use a hatchet to remove a fly from your friend's forehead."
> —CHINESE PROVERB

When you begin to cross-pollinate, you learn from other people, and that broadens you in life. You need diversity without duplication. All fruitful relationships are the result of exchanging strength and not duplicating them. If you will overcome your insecurities and intimidations, there are people whom God wants to put in your life because they are trained in areas where you are not. They will actually cause a maturing in your life to fulfill what God has for you.

Here are a few examples from my life. About thirty

some years ago, I had no idea of what "healthy" or nutritious meant, because no one had taught me how to eat wisely. All I knew was southern fried food. I mean, I didn't use a tablespoon of Crisco. I used the whole thing. My corn had more butter than it had corn. And I didn't eat cornbread unless I had at least a bowl of gravy on top. I often lacked energy and had a rundown immune system. If God had not brought the right people into my life, I know I wouldn't have the physical strength or stamina to do what I'm doing today.

> "Trust is to human relationships what faith is to gospel living. It is the beginning place, the foundation upon which more can be built. Where trust is, love can flourish."
>
> —BARBARA B. SMITH

At that same time, I wore outfits that did not "flatter" my body style or complement the "occasion" I was attending. I thought that "doing your nails" meant washing your hands. I could continue, but you get the picture. I had little knowledge because of my limited exposure.

But God had a plan, so He began to send women into my life to mentor and train and teach me how to dress and take care of my nails and how to talk. If I had stayed insecure and intimidated and not cross-pollinated, I would never have been able to go where God wanted to take me. I had to learn from other people, because they had been exposed to aspects of life that I had not been. God graciously put me in situations where I could be trained to fulfill what God has for me.

All relationships are investments. They require time and energy, and they yield returns. If a preacher, for instance, will interact with a skilled counselor, he can become much more effective by learning new communication skills with people. We need to interact. We need diversity. It is others' diversity that will sharpen and bring good things out of you.

While you need diversity, you also must have common direction—common values and goals. Diversity is only good when you're going in the same direction with someone. Ultimately, if that person is going north and you're going south, you're going to miss it. It is vital to find out if the person you are joining yourself to has the same destination. The real foundation needs to be, "Are we headed in the same direction with the same destination?" Because if their vision leads you one way, and your vision leads another way, there is ultimately going to be a fork in the road.

If you have found someone whom you are considering for marriage, you need to ask them, "Where do you want to end up in life?" It is extremely important where that person is going to end up while you discover together how to get there. If the two of you are going to end up in the same place, you will do the best you can to figure out the journey together. Two people grow together by establishing mutual goals and working to achieve them. Interestingly, it is the journey toward the goals and not the goals themselves that help the relationship grow and bond. But if that person wants to end up at one spot, and you are heading for another spot, this is not the person with whom you are to connect.

Having the same deliberate direction is so vital when you begin to form partnerships and relationships and covenants. I need to remind you of Amos 3:3: "Can two walk together, unless they are agreed?" To *agree* means "to meet by appointment" or "to have a deliberate summons." In other words, unless we meet by appointment and deliberately come together, we will end up going in different directions.

The apostle Paul said, "I, therefore, the prisoner of the Lord, beseech you to walk worthy of the calling with which you were called, with all lowliness and gentleness, with long suffering, bearing with one another in love, endeavoring to keep the unity of the Spirit in the bond of peace" (Ephesians 4:1–3). He is telling us how to and with what attitude to make every effort to keep and guard the unity, the oneness of the Spirit in the bond of peace. You are to work diligently at keeping unity with the people whom you are in relationship with. Staying in unity takes effort and negotiations. If you allow it, life will throw all sorts of divisive wedges within relationships. You have to deliberately stay on the same page, which means to stay in step or synchronization with one another, whether it involves a business, a friendship, or your marriage. This is where you create harmony.

For this to occur, you will come to a place called negotiation, because in life you will have to make some compromises in order to stay in the spirit of unity. The Bible says, "Do not let the sun go down on your wrath" (Ephesians 4:26). In other words, resolve quickly and without hesitation any conflict where there is potential for division. Not everything is worth a battle. When you go to war, make sure there are spoils and they are worth the price that has been paid in battle. It is wise to choose your battles and figure out which ones you should take on. Don't simply fight for the sake of fighting when peace and unity are an option.

Conclusion

These are the questions you need to answer:

1. *Is your life filled with diverse people who are committed to a common goal?*
2. *Is your life filled with people who are challenging you and stretching you, but who have the same destination and common goals as you do?*
3. *Have you surrendered yourself to a team of traveling companions who include your well-being as a priority?*
4. *Do your relationships raise you up along the road to success or are they keeping you in a place that's stagnant?*

Find ways to challenge and stimulate growth within your existing relationships. Help cultivate and develop one another while traveling to your destination.

Key #8
to Healthy Relationships
Keep the Big Picture in Mind When You Experience Trials in Your Relationships

All relationships go through trials. You must constantly ask yourself about motives and the bigger picture when you experience trials and testings in your relationships. All relationships hit speed bumps; occasionally some of them hit mountains. Some relationships just have train wrecks.

Your family is going to go through trials. You'll face countless trials on your job. Are you going to forfeit the place where God has planted you just because you are going through a difficult time, or will you stand in perseverance? To persevere means you stay in the same place regardless of the difficulties. It is to be stationary and steadfast. At different times, life will press you into places where you won't think you have what it takes to make it. Remember that tough times don't last, but tough people do. When your determination is fixed, don't despair. Great works are not always performed by strength but by perseverance.

So here are four Cs to help you work through the trials of relationships. You have to *confront*, to *correct*, to *compromise*, and, if none of those work, you have to *cut it off*.

God is using that struggle and hardship to work for you and not against you. God is using difficulties with other people to sharpen you. God is using them to bring long suffering into your life. Long suffering is a fruit of the Spirit (Galatians 5:22). It means to endure or stand firm under pressure through the process with an assurance that God's promises are going to come to pass in your life.

When you face trying times in a relationship, there are several things to help you work through it that I want to share with you. There are occasions when you have to confront. Confrontation is healthy; it's not a negative thing. Some of you are starting to tremble right now because you're thinking, Confrontation, negative—yelling! No, that's not what confrontation means. It simply means to see others clearly and face directly what really is true about your relationship. Confrontation helps uncover the reality of the relationship.

And when you confront, you need to do so in God's timing. There's timing to everything. Be conscious of the time that you choose for confrontation. Remember: you are to always be in control of your actions and decisions. In other words, you don't confront when you're acting like beast woman because you're over hormonal. That is not confrontation. That is you having a crazy day and needing a release valve.

Here's what you do. You look at the big picture; you look at everything. You take in the facts. You digest them. Don't make a permanent decision in a temporary situation. You gather all the information because you can't make a quality decision with limited information. After you gather all the information, you look at the reality of the relationship, prayerfully asking God for wisdom and guidance.

There are some wise techniques to use in confrontation. One of them is called the sandwich technique, where when you talk to people you use statements that enforce something positive, then negative, and then positive. Whatever you are confronting that person with, you sandwich it in between a positive beginning and a positive ending. The reasoning behind this technique is that it helps keep the person from immediately getting on the defense. This is especially beneficial when a person has been accustomed to receiving criticism that they experience as rejection. Every time they erred, critical parents or teachers would pass on judgment. Because it can be so painful, many strategies get developed to minimize the hurts being experienced. These strategies are all part of a "defense mechanism" so as not to feel the hurt and pain. However, without learning to resolve and work through these barriers, there can be serious disruption to your relations with others. Constructive criticism can help you improve yourself. When you make a mistake, feedback will help you learn how to not repeat the same thing. When God confronts us, He brings out good things to us, reveals His correction to us, and then uplifts us through His edification and encouragement.

> "The quality of your life is the quality of relationships."
> —ANTHONY ROBBIN

Confrontation does not mean just bringing up something that concerns you about the person. To confront means being honest and transparent about yourself to the other person. It can be painful to be honest about the issues God wants to deal with in your life, but it yields a good result in the long term. All of us have weaknesses and issues that we continually deal with. That does not make you "bad" or "less"; it simply means you are "human."

If you just sweep everything under the rug, it can be unhealthy. Ask God for the wisdom as to how, where, and when to confront.

There also has to be compromise and cooperation to resolve conflicting needs in relationships. I like it when people don't tell me what they think I want to hear, but they tell me what I need to hear. The most beneficial people in my life are the ones who say what needs to be said out of a motivation of genuine love and concern.

A wise man said an "open rebuke is better than love

carefully concealed" (Proverbs 27:5). An honest and gentle rebuke, motivated by love, increases trust, commitment, and integrity in both the giver and the receiver.

The same is true in our relationship with God. "If you endure chastening, God deals with you as with sons; for what son is there whom a father does not chasten? But if you are without chastening, of which all have become partakers, then you are illegitimate and not sons" (Hebrews 12:7–8). God says, "If you can't stay under my instruction and disciplinary correction, you're not even a son of mine." This is part of our relationship with Him. It is for our benefit and not our detriment. You need people who are motivated by love to speak the truth you need to hear and not tell you just what you want to hear in order to grow and develop.

You need people who don't control you, but who can speak clarity in your life with love and pure motives. For that to happen, you have to be submitted in relationship. You can never truly have discipleship without relationship, because discipleship without relationship produces rebellion. But when you have relationship, you recognize that person speaking into your life loves you and has your best interests in mind. When they speak into your life, it will prevent you from missing the mark on so many different things.

You need to start asking God to bring the right people into your life. How does God speak to us? God doesn't sit in heaven and yell, "Hey, you!" That's not how He does it. He usually speaks through people. He brings people into our life to whom we open our heart in a submitted covenant relationship. We need people whom we have relationship with in our life who hold us accountable and remind us of our attitudes, our conversations, our thoughts, for everything in our life.

I don't want to always travel and never get anywhere. That's why I believe in building relationships that have open lines of communication to say, "Paula, get your attitude right." Therefore, I have people in my life to whom I have said, "If I start speaking in this way, or if I start getting negative, or you see me doing this or that, you'd better not let me stay like that. Please speak into my life. Don't see danger and not tell me about it. Love me enough to not tell me what you think I want to hear. Tell me what I need to hear so I don't miss what God has for me."

This has to be birthed out of love. You can't speak into somebody's life when you don't have a relationship with them that has love as its foundation. The Bible says, "Hatred stirs up strife, but love covers all sins" (Proverbs 10:12). "To cover" does not mean to hide. It means "love prevents all sins." When I know you love me, you can speak anything to me because you are not out there to hurt me. You're there for my benefit.

Everything in relationships is about negotiation. Negotiation is learning to negotiate, and negotiation is win, win. When you learn the art of negotiation, you don't always have to be right. It means you compromise in some areas so you prevent conflict in other areas. This often means seeing things through the eyes of the others involved in the situation or the problem. Empathy helps you understand your partners' position more clearly. Healthy compromise is the hallmark of healthy relationships.

> **"Let us be grateful to people who make us happy. They are the charming gardeners who make our souls blossom."**
> —MARCEL PROUST

There are some relationships that you need to cut off. As I said previously, when you have attempted in every manner to have a functional relationship, and it continues to not only fail but becomes detrimental to your well-being, you must seriously examine ending the relationship. It's lethal when you are surrounded by people who have an attitude of indifference toward you, and they don't have your best personal interests in mind—they don't really care about, nurture, or love you. You must cut those relationships off in your life.

It is dangerous when you are with someone who is deceptive, destructive, and harmful. Walking away does not always mean a complete severance. Every situation is different and must be carefully considered when making decisions. However, the ending of a relationship does not mean the ending of you. You are not "over" or finished because your relationship is ending. Love yourself enough to know when to say this is destructive to your well-being and/or those whom you care about and love. Find the courage and faith to trust God for your future.

KEY #9
to Healthy Relationships

Find People Who Share Your Passion

Partnership is at its optimum when you partner with people who share the same intensity and the same objectives you have. Both are needed. You need passion and an intensity of focus that fuels that relationship and the objectives you desire to achieve together. Do we see the same way? Can we get there together? Do we share the same value system?

You need intensity, because intensity helps you focus on how much you desire to reach your goals. It is imperative that you have clarity regarding what you want, and you need intensity of desire to accompany it.

Here's an example from a family. You and your wife want to move out of the apartment and get into a house of your own. You want to be able to provide your children with an inheritance and put them through college. That's the objective. But how badly do you want it? That's what really counts, because if you and your spouse really want it, you'll sacrifice something today so you can have a better tomorrow. But if the two of you don't really want it, then one of you is going to go out and buy a $300 dress on a credit card that you're paying 21 percent interest on, and it's going to take you 12 years to pay that off. The desire for a house wasn't intense enough to put you into the house.

So your objective and your intensity of desire have to be the same. That takes us back to compromise. What is it you want? How much? You can rate how much you desire it. For example, you say you want God in your marriage. That's the objective. But do you really? Does the intensity of your desire for God mean you are willing to pray together for ten minutes a day? Are you willing to go and do a Bible study together? Are you willing to go to church together?

Intensity has to do with desire. You never reach your objectives and goals without the desire to do so. Without desire and intensity you live in a place called complacency. And as long as you are complacent, you won't get there. Passive people don't win in life. You have to want it because the desire is the fuel that gets you to the place God wants you to go.

So once you get your objectives clear, whether it's for your company, your ministry, your marriage, or your friendships, you have to rate the level of intensity. If you want something at a 10, and your spouse wants something at a 1, then you balance out at a 5. But if you want it at a 9, and your friend wants it at an 8, that becomes the priority on your list because intensity has to do with desire, which is passion. Without passion you don't have the fuel to ever fulfill the objective you have set before you.

You can't build a life without the goals. You cannot give the goals the fuel they need without the desire being there. People who really want something find a way and don't make excuses. You say you want to be a man or woman of God. Really? Then you find a way. If you don't, you find an excuse. Intensity—how badly do you want it?

The same is true of your prayer life. Your prayers get answered according to your desire. "Therefore I say to you, whatever things you ask when you pray, believe that you receive them, and you will have them" (Mark 11:24). The ability to press into prayer has to do with the amount of desire in your life. If you want something badly enough, you find a way.

Intensity has a lot to do with your fulfilling the objectives and goals in relationships. It causes you to press through boundaries and barriers.

CHAPTER NINE

Steps *to* Interdependence

The goal of a healthy relationship is to be interdependent. Interdependence is about making friends and allies and forming partnerships, connections with other people that reciprocate benefits. Mutual respect, trust, loyalty, integrity, honor, and value are all descriptive words of interdependence. When two people depend on each other equally, it is an interdependent and healthy relationship.

I am free to be me; you are free to be you.

I celebrate your uniqueness; you celebrate my uniqueness.

I grow as an individual; you grow as an individual.

And together we're going to have a healthy relationship, whether it is a working one, a spiritual one, an intimate one, or a friendship.

We're healthy; we're interdependent.

It means you want to benefit one from the other. It means you cross-pollinate, and you recognize they have strengths you don't have, that you can learn from each other. Iron sharpens iron (Proverbs 27:17). You don't want to be relying on it, but you want to be reliable to it.

And in order to receive those benefits of a healthy relationship, there are six major steps to building interdependence. Remember, though, *love is the foundation.* You find the love of God, you love yourself, and then you begin to love others.

STEP #1
Get to Know and Understand the Other Person

Relationships thrive as you get to know and understand the other person—their values and who they are—and appreciate their individuality. Recognize that God created them in the same way He created you—fearfully and wonderfully. And even though they are not just like you doesn't mean they are not fearfully and wonderfully made. They have their own uniqueness. Understand that individual for who they are. Get to know that individual and enjoy the discovery of their uniqueness.

Studies have shown that in long-lasting, satisfying, fulfilling relationships the individuals never stop seeking to know one another. They do not assume they know what the other person is thinking or feeling. Instead, they determine to pay close attention to the details. They notice the small changes that might easily be taken for granted. The power to "know" doesn't say, "I have you figured out, follow me." Rather, it says, "Tell me about yourself." When you stop knowing, you stop growing.

STEP #2
Attend to the Little Things in the Relationship

You need to attend to the little things in the relationship. Scripture says, "Do not despise these small beginnings" (Zechariah 4:10 NLT). What it's saying is, watch the details. When you begin to attend to the details in relationships, they become big things. Pay attention to the small things, because they make a big difference. Remember, it is a small hinge that swings a big door.

STEP #3
Clarify Your Expectations

Clarify your expectations in the relationship. Nobody is a mind reader except for God. Learn how to communicate in your relationships. Communication is a two-way collaborative process. Listening is the most important of all the communication skills that can create and preserve intimacy. When you listen well, you understand the person better, and you know without mind reading why he/she says and does things. Most difficulties that come up are rooted in ambiguous talk where you are assuming you know what the other person is thinking. Instead, tell the other person what you thought you heard and begin asking questions in a noninterrogative manner to clarify

God is a God who is very clear in His communication with us. "Then the LORD answered me and said: 'Write the vision and make it plain on tablets, that he may run who reads it' " (Habakkuk 2:2). How does the Lord say to make the communication of the vision? "Plain." It needs to be clear so the reader can "run" with it. How can I run with something I don't understand or even know the direction of it?

When we're in a relationship, whether it regards work or our marriage or a friendship, we have expectations and desires that need to be stated, not demanded, clearly. How many friendships have been damaged over something as small as one person not giving the other person the time they expected? Just say, "Here's what I have. I have an hour on Friday, and I'd like to meet you for coffee to spend it with you." Speak out the desire clearly. Don't assume the other person is going to know what you want. Offer what you have and what you would like, and go from there.

STEP #4
Show Personal Integrity in All of Your Relationships

Show personal integrity at all times in your relationships. For interdependence to work in your relationships, you cannot live to please the other person nor can they live to please you (that is codependence). Rather, you are committed to living according to the convictions and values you believe God has given you, and the other person is free to do the same. We are both mature enough to realize there are some fundamental truths in the Word of God that are very obvious, but there are other life issues about which the Bible is silent. Although our convictions on these issues may differ, we are committed to being true to what we believe and pleasing God by not compromising our position.

> "Treasure your relationships, not your possessions."
> —ANTHONY D'ANGELO

I teach my children that I live with something called "PI." Other people may agree or disagree with some of the convictions I have. I cannot tell them they must share my convictions, and they cannot tell me I must share their convictions. But at the end of my life, when I stand before God, I will stand there alone. So the Bible says, "Work out your own salvation with fear and trembling" (Philippians 2:12).

And so at the end of the day, when I lay my head on my pillow, I ask myself, "Paula, are you okay with everything you decided today? Is your "Personal Integrity" intact? Were you true to your personal convictions? Have you done what you felt God wanted you to do for this day? Were you authentic to yourself and pleasing to God for this day?" When you live with personal integrity, you can lay your head down in bed and truly enter into rest. You'll not be tormented on the inside because there's been a disconnect between living in alignment with your convictions and value system and trying to be something to somebody else that you really aren't.

STEP #5
Learn to Apologize

When you've done something wrong in a relationship, admit you're wrong. Humble yourself and apologize sincerely. Go to your children and apologize when you blow it. When my children were growing up, I wanted to do right, but I didn't always know how to do right. And I just missed it sometimes. And when I missed it, I wasn't so prideful or so arrogant to stand up and act like I had it all together. Such has been the case in every role I have functioned in. I have done things to the best of my ability with the knowledge I had at the time.

I have even gone before my congregation and said, "Guys, I missed it." I remember when we first started the ladies ministry in our church, I put a precious lady, who had the gift of teaching and was much older in the Lord than I was, in the main position. I was not seasoned and lacked her maturity, and truth to tell, I was too intimidated to fulfill the role so I put her in that position. But I knew it was out of order. I knew God wanted me to be leading that ministry position, but I was struggling. And no matter how hard we tried, the women's ministry wouldn't grow, and it wasn't right.

I allowed the ministry to languish for six months. It was frustrating and chaotic, because whenever something is out of order, there won't be peace and a flow to it. It had nothing to do with the godly lady I'd put in charge. It was me. Eventually, I had to go and say to my ladies, "I'm sorry. I missed it. I missed God." And even worse, I had to take that precious woman out of her position and say to her, "Please forgive me. I'm sorry, because I missed it." It was actually a great relief to her as well.

So don't be so prideful or insecure. Say, "I'm sorry." Give yourself permission to be human. When you blow it, admit it and fix what is fixable. Ask for forgiveness when necessary, and move on.

One Final Word

Perhaps as you were reading this book you asked the question: "Paula, what qualifies you to talk about healthy relationships? Are you a psychologist or a counselor?"

That's a fair question. Some psychiatrists would review my past and say that I should be locked up in a mental institute and in need of medication or lifelong therapy. That is until an extensive evaluation is performed and then they would discover the wholeness which has occurred through the transformative power of God and His word which changed me from the inside to the outside and continues to do so to this day. I remember a counselor early on in my life who said, "There's no hope for her." Sexually and physically abused. Eating disorders. Poverty. Dysfunction after dysfunction. Displacement, rejection and abandonment issues. "Are you even whole, Paula?"

What qualifies me? Day after day after day of taking the Word of God as a mirror for my life. His Word rightly reflects and tells us the truth. I allowed the Word of God to show me everything in my life that was a lie and everything that is truth. I continue to do that as I discover new truths every day. Each day is an opportunity for growth and transformation. As you grow from the Word of God, you are challenged with the realization of how much progress has occurred and how much still needs to happen. One philosopher said, ". . . I am the wisest man of all. . . . I have discovered that I know nothing." This is a lifelong journey with God and one that is well worth it to live Happy, Healthy and Whole.

As you know the Word, do the Word, speak the Word, then you make your way successful and you make your way prosperous. Much success to you in every area of your life.

Three of Paula's Most Popular Books

Something Greater There is something in each of us that tells us we were created for a greater purpose. However, life's pain, difficulties, and setbacks can overwhelm us and destroy our sense of destiny. Through personal accounts of heartbreak, childhood abuse, and midlife devastation Paula reveals how by surrendering to God's purpose for her life and refusing to quit she became an overcomer and you can too! Vulnerable, honest and inspiring.

Move On, Move Up Do you want to move on but you don't know how? Do you want to move up but can't find help? Paula offers hope filled insights, practical applications and key passages of scripture that will equip you to discover the purpose of your pain & how to overcome any challenge that crosses your path. Don't give up!

Dare to Dream Through real life illustrations, personal stories and stirring insights Paula reveals the keys to healing, hope and identity. She shows you how to become an expert on the subject of YOU, see yourself as God sees you & teaches you how to embrace a lifetime of discovery and transformation. Don't stop dreaming.

Get your copy wherever books are sold or by visiting the store at paulawhite.org. Many more titles are available.